The Integrated Approach to Arabic Instruction

Leading teacher of Arabic, Munther Younes, explores the realities of teaching Arabic as a foreign language (AFL) and outlines his groundbreaking approach to instruction, tried and tested over many years at Cornell University.

The Integrated Approach to Arabic Instruction introduces teachers to the features of an integrated Arabic program – one that simultaneously teaches the two varieties of the language, Modern Standard Written Arabic, *Fuṣḥā*, and the dialect, *ʿĀmmiyya*, in a way that reflects the authentic practice of native Arabic speakers. This pedagogy, Younes argues, is the most logical, effective and economical method of instruction as it prepares students fully for the realities of the Arabic diglossic situation.

Younes takes teachers through the following areas:

- consideration of the current Arabic sociolinguistic situation and key debates in the field;
- outline of changing student goals and the needs of the modern AFL learner;
- overview of the Integrated Approach covering its rationale, features, implementation methods and usage of instructional materials in the classroom;
- response to objections to the Integrated Approach, outlining its advantages over alternative practices and clarifying crucial issues in practice.

The Integrated Approach to Arabic Instruction addresses a pressing issue deeply relevant to the world of Arabic language instruction, placed in the practical context of shifting attitudes among students and educators. It will be an essential resource for all teachers of Arabic as a Foreign Language.

Munther Younes is Reis Senior Lecturer of Arabic Language and Linguistics and Director of the Arabic Program in the Department of Near Eastern Studies at Cornell University, USA. His publications include the pioneering three-part textbook series ʿArabiyyat al-Naas (2014), *The Routledge Introduction to Qur'anic Arabic* (2013) and *Kalila wa Dimna for Students of Arabic* (2013), all published with Routledge.

Related titles

'Arabiyyat al-Naas (Part One): An Introductory Course in Arabic
Munther Younes, Makda Weatherspoon and Maha Saliba Foster
978-0-415-51693-8

'Arabiyyat al-Naas (Part Two): An Intermediate Course in Arabic
Munther Younes and Hanada Al-Masri
978-0-415-50908-4

'Arabiyyat al-Naas (Part Three): An Advanced Course in Arabic
Munther Younes and Yomna Chami
978-0-415-50901-5

"Anyone who has seen what Munther's students can do in Arabic knows that his Integrated Approach is decidedly successful. This book begins with a rigorous overview of past research about variation in Arabic. It then provides convincing argumentation in favor of adopting an Integrated Approach along with actual examples. Finally, it debunks opposition and shows that the Integrated Approach meets our students' needs by reflecting the sociolinguistic realities of the Arabic-speaking world."

Jeremy Palmer, *American University of Sharjah, UAE*

"*The Integrated Approach to Arabic Instruction* provides a concise yet comprehensive overview of the linguistic research that supports using the Integrated Approach in the teaching of Arabic as a foreign language. This book presents the best methodology that successful Arabic programs should adopt to meet the aspirations of a growing community of Arabic language learners and educators."

Mohammad Al-Masri, *University of Oklahoma, USA*

The Integrated Approach to Arabic Instruction

Munther Younes

Routledge
Taylor & Francis Group
LONDON AND NEW YORK

First published 2015
by Routledge
2 Park Square, Milton Park, Abingdon, Oxon OX14 4RN

and by Routledge
711 Third Avenue, New York, NY 10017

Routledge is an imprint of the Taylor & Francis Group, an informa business

British Library Cataloguing in Publication Data
A catalogue record for this book is available from the British Library

Library of Congress Cataloging in Publication Data
Younes, Munther Abdullatif, 1952- author.
The integrated approach to Arabic instruction / Munther Younes.
pages cm
Arabic and English.
Includes bibliographical references and index.
1. Arabic language--Study and teaching--Foreign speakers. 2. Arabic language--Spoken Arabic. 3. Arabic language--Grammar--Study and teaching. 4. Language experience approach in education. I. Title.
PJ6065.Y68 2015
492.7071'1--dc23

2014021688

ISBN: 978-1-138-82230-6 (hbk)
ISBN: 978-1-138-82232-0 (pbk)
ISBN: 978-1-315-74061-4 (ebk)

Typeset in Times New Roman
by Taylor & Francis Books

Contents

Acknowledgments vii

Introduction 1

1 The Arabic Sociolinguistic Situation 2
Diglossia according to Ferguson 2
Challenges to Ferguson's analysis 5
Fuṣḥā *or* ʿĀmmiyya *base? 11*
The Fuṣḥā-ʿĀmmiyya *continuum 12*
Other aspects of the Arabic language situation 12
Summary and conclusions 15

2 Changing Student Goals 22
The early days of Arabic study 22
Modern Standard Arabic and the "Orange Books" 23
The proficiency movement: new student needs 24

3 Responding to the Needs of the Modern AFL Learner 26
Fuṣḥā *only or primarily 26*
Reasons for privileging Fuṣḥā *26*
Consequences of privileging Fuṣḥā *28*

4 Integration 31
What is "integration"? 31
Integration: rationale and basic description 32
Implementation 33
The ʿĀmmiyya *component 34*
What is Levantine Educated Spoken Arabic (LESA)? 34
Writing LESA 37
Why integration makes sense 38

5 Objections to Integration 46
Which dialect? 46
Previous attempts at introducing ESA in the Arabic classroom 47

Badawi on the teaching of ESA and MSA 48
Why LESA? 49
Dialect-neutrality 50
Student testimonials 50
How many dialects should a student learn? 53
Can a teacher teach a dialect that is not his or her own? 53
Confusion 54

6 Conclusion 57

References 59
Index 64

Acknowledgments

I would like to take this opportunity to thank the Routledge team, who have demonstrated the utmost professionalism and dedication throughout this project. In particular, I am grateful to Andrea Hartill, Publisher in Language Learning; Isabelle Cheng, Senior Editorial Assistant, Colloquials and Language Learning; and Sarah May, Deputy Production Editorial Manager, Humanities. Their continuous and unwavering support in the publication of the *'Arabiyyat al-Naas* textbook series and their belief in and enthusiasm for the Integrated Approach to Arabic instruction were truly inspiring. I will always be in their debt.

I would also like to thank the two anonymous reviewers of an earlier manuscript of the book who made a number of valuable comments that I hope have contributed to improving the quality of the final product.

Finally, I would like to dedicate this book to the memory of my friend and colleague, the late Michel Nicola of the Defense Language Institute in Monterey, California. It was through discussions with him in the late 1980s that the idea of the Integrated Approach was born.

Introduction

The field of teaching Arabic as a foreign language (TAFL) has been plagued by a set of problems resulting from the sociolinguistic phenomenon known as *diglossia*, i.e. the existence side by side of two varieties of the language that are used each in a specific set of situations. According to Ryding (1991: 214), "[T]his long-standing paradigm of dichotomy or sharp cleavage between literary and colloquial Arabic has both weakened the effectiveness of Arabic language teaching and undermined the appeal of Arabic as a learnable and useful foreign language, thus leaving the field in crisis for many years."

The main goal of this book is to introduce the reader to the main features of an integrated Arabic program, one that introduces the two varieties of the languages, called here *Fuṣḥā* and *ʿĀmmiyya*, simultaneously and in a way that reflects the use of the language by Arabic native speakers. It will be argued that this integration is the most logical, effective, and economical way to prepare the student of Arabic as a foreign language to deal successfully with the Arabic diglossic situation.

The book is divided into five chapters. The first chapter presents an overview of the Arabic sociolinguistic situation, with a focus on diglossia because of its centrality to the main goal of the book. In the second chapter I discuss the changing needs of Arabic-as-a-foreign-language students, with a focus on the needs of the present generation of Arabic learners in a university setting. The third chapter considers the generally unsatisfactory institutional response to these needs. The fourth chapter presents the "Integrated Approach", its rationale, main features, implementation in Arabic instructional materials and in the Arabic classroom as well as its advantages over alternative practices. The fifth and final chapter focuses on the objections traditionally raised against the Integrated Approach and a response to these objections.

1 The Arabic Sociolinguistic Situation

No scholarly work on Arabic linguistics published in the English-speaking world in the twentieth century has generated more interest and controversy than Charles Ferguson's "Diglossia" paper (Ferguson 1959). According to Ferguson (Ferguson 1996: 49), since the publication of the paper in 1959, "hundreds of articles and a score of books have been published on the topic of diglossia, most of them referring directly to the 1959 paper ... ". In spite of the criticism it has been subjected to by Arabic linguists, its basic insights about the Arabic sociolinguistic situation are as valid in the second decade of the twenty-first century as they were sixty years before (Bassiouney 2009: 13). In the following paragraphs, I will summarize those insights that are directly relevant to the main goal of this book, which is to present a program for teaching Arabic to the foreign learner that takes into account the realities of the Arabic sociolinguistic situation, particularly the phenomenon of "diglossia", a term that owes its widespread use in the field to Ferguson.

Diglossia according to Ferguson

Characterizing the Arabic sociolinguistic situation as "diglossic", along with Modern Greek, Swiss German, and Haitian Creole, Ferguson defines diglossia as follows:

> a relatively stable language situation in which, in addition to the primary dialects of the language (which may include a standard or regional standards), there is a very divergent, highly codified (often grammatically more complex) superposed variety, the vehicle of a large and respected body of written literature, either of an earlier period or in another speech community, which is learned largely by formal education and is used for most written and formal spoken purposes but is not used by any sector of the community for ordinary conversation.

Ferguson refers to the superposed variety as high (H) and to the primary dialects as low (L). In the case of Arabic, Ferguson's H corresponds to what is known in Arabic as *Fuṣḥā*, a term that includes both Modern Standard Arabic (MSA) and its older form, Classical Arabic (CA), and his L corresponds to the Arabic colloquial dialects.

According to Ferguson, diglossic language situations differ from standard-with-dialects situations in a number of areas, which include the following:

Function

Each of the two varieties serves specific functions. "In one set of situations, only H is appropriate, and in another only L, with the two sets overlapping only very slightly" (Ferguson 1959: 328). For example, a sermon in a church or mosque, a university lecture, a personal letter, a news broadcast are normally given (or written) in H, but conversations with family and friends, soap operas, and folk literature are conducted in L (ibid.: 329).

Ferguson notes the importance of using the right variety in the right situation:

> … an outsider who learns to speak fluent, accurate L and then uses it in a formal speech is an object of ridicule. A member of the speech community who uses H in a purely conversational situation or in an informal activity like shopping is equally an object of ridicule … it is typical behavior to have someone read aloud from a newspaper written in H and then proceed to discuss the contents in L … and to listen to a formal speech in H and then discuss it, often with the speaker himself, in L.
>
> (Ibid.)

Ferguson adds: " … proverbs, politeness formulas, and the like are in H even when cited in ordinary conversation by illiterates" (ibid.).

Prestige

> [T]he speakers regard H as superior to L … there is usually a belief that H is somehow more beautiful, more logical, better able to express important thoughts … . In some cases the superiority of H is connected with religion … . For Arabic, H is the language of the Qur'an … and as such is widely believed to constitute the actual words of God … .
>
> (Ibid.: 330)

Literary heritage

> [T]here is a sizable body of written literature in H which is held in high esteem by the speech community … .
>
> (Ibid.)

Acquisition

> L is invariably learned by children in what may be regarded as the "normal" way of learning one's mother tongue ... [but] the actual learning of H is chiefly accomplished by the means of formal education ... . The speaker is at home in L to a degree he almost never achieves in H. The grammatical structure of L is learned without explicit discussion of grammatical concepts; the grammar of H is learned in terms of "rules" and norms to be imitated.
>
> (Ibid.: 331)

Standardization

> [T]here is a strong tradition of grammatical study of the H form of the language ... . By contrast, descriptive and normative studies of the L form are either non-existent or relatively recent and slight in quantity. Often they have been carried out first or chiefly by scholars outside the speech community and are written in other languages. There is no settled orthography and there is wide variation in pronunciation, grammar, and vocabulary ... . In the Arabic speech community ... regional standards exist such as the Arabic of Cairo.
>
> (Ibid.: 331, 332)

Stability

> Diglossia typically persists at least several centuries ... it can last well over a thousand years. The communicative tensions which arise in the diglossia situation may be resolved by the use of relatively un-codified, unstable, intermediate forms of the language (*al-lugha al-wusṭā*) ... which is a kind of spoken Arabic much used in certain semiformal or cross-dialectal situations [and which] has a highly classical vocabulary with few or no inflectional endings, with certain features of classical syntax, but with a fundamentally colloquial base in morphology and syntax, and a generous admixture of colloquial vocabulary.
>
> (Ibid.: 332)

Grammar

> H has grammatical categories not present in L and has an inflectional system of nouns and verbs which is much reduced or totally absent in L ... .
>
> (Ibid.: 333)

> [T]he grammatical structure of any given L variety is simpler than that of its corresponding H.
>
> (Ibid.: 334)

Lexicon

> Generally speaking, the bulk of the vocabulary of H and L is shared, of course with variations in form and with differences of use and meaning.
>
> (Ibid.)

Commenting on the differences between diglossic language situations and situations with a standard and dialects, Ferguson writes that:

> no segment of the speech community in diglossia regularly uses H as a medium of ordinary conversation, and any attempt to do so is felt to be ... pedantic and artificial ... . In the more usual standard-with-dialects situation the standard is often similar to the variety of a certain region or social group, which is used in ordinary conversation more or less naturally by members of the group as a superposed variety by others.
>
> (Ibid.: 336–7)

Finally, Ferguson points out that:

> The proponents of H argue that H must be adopted because it connects the community with its glorious past or with the world community and because it is a naturally unifying factor, as opposed to the divisive nature of the L dialects.
>
> (Ibid.: 338–9)

Challenges to Ferguson's analysis

Ferguson's analysis of the Arabic language situation has been challenged by several linguists on a number of grounds, particularly the following: (1) the inadequacy of a two-way dichotomy is to account for the complexities of this situation; (2) the inaccuracy of the distribution of functions between the H variety, i.e. *Fuṣḥā*, and the L variety (the colloquial dialects); and (3) Ferguson's assumptions about the prestige of *Fuṣḥā* in comparison with the dialects.

The inadequacy of the two varieties

Blanc's five levels

The first major challenge came in the form of a study "encouraged" and "prodded into existence" by Ferguson himself (Blanc 1960: 86). Blanc analyzed an audio recording done at the Army Language School in Monterey (California) of inter-dialectal speech by four educated native speakers of Arabic (two from Baghdad, one from Aleppo and one from Jerusalem). On the basis of this analysis, he identified five levels along the Classical-colloquial continuum (ibid.: 85): (1) plain colloquial, (2) koineized colloquial, (3) semi-literary, (4) modified classical, and (5) standard classical. He states that,

> once one gets beyond homespun conversation in relaxed colloquial within a single dialect, it is the exception rather than the rule to find any sustained segment of discourse in a single one of the style varieties alluded to. Speakers tend to pass from one to the other, sometimes within a single sentence, so that over-all stylistic characterization of a given segment of discourse is a complex and delicate matter … .
>
> (Ibid.)

Using what Blanc calls "leveling" and "classicizing" devices (ibid.: 81–2), Arabic speakers modify their speech to accommodate speakers of other dialects. As an illustration of "leveling", Blanc gives the example of Palestinians from the countryside who replace their *ch* sound with *k* in imitation of speakers from Jerusalem and other urban centers, as in *chalb/kalb*, 'dog'.

Classicizing devices involve borrowing items and linguistic features from Classical Arabic, as in Cairene *qism* used to replace of *'ism*, 'police station'

Some of Blanc's conclusions support Ferguson's analysis. For example, he states that in his sample of inter-dialectal conversation, "Dialectal features remain strikingly predominant in the phonology and grammar, somewhat less so in the lexicon … , [the speakers'] idiom is not midway between classical and colloquial, but unequivocally much closer to colloquial" (ibid.: 91). He adds, "[T]he morphology is essentially dialectal" (ibid.: 92). These statements echo Ferguson's regarding the existence of "a kind of spoken Arabic much used in certain semiformal or cross-dialectal situations [which] has a highly classical vocabulary with few or no inflectional endings, with certain features of classical syntax, but with a fundamentally colloquial base in morphology and syntax … " (Ferguson 1959: 332).

Badawi's five levels

In his classic sociolinguistic study of Arabic as used in contemporary Egypt, Badawi (1973) also identified five levels along the *Fuṣḥā*/colloquial or H/L continuum in every fully functioning linguistic community (*mujtama' lughawī mutakāmil*) in contemporary Egypt (1973: 89):

1 *Fuṣḥā al-turāth* (*Fuṣḥā* of the [Arab/Islamic] heritage): traditional or classical *Fuṣḥā*, with relatively no outside influence;
2 *Fuṣḥā al-'Aṣr* (contemporary *Fuṣḥā*): *Fuṣḥā* that is particularly influenced by contemporary civilization;
3 *'Āmmiyyat al-muthaqqafīn* (vernacular of the cultured, educated): colloquial language that is influenced by *Fuṣḥā* and contemporary civilization;
4 *'Āmmiyyat al-mutanawwirīn* (vernacular of the enlightened, literate): colloquial language influenced by modern civilization;

5 *ʿĀmmiyyat al-'ummiyyīn* (vernacular of the illiterate): colloquial language that is not influenced by *Fuṣḥā* or modern civilization.

Badawi defines each of these levels and describes their usage, emphasizing the oral part of each as used in different Egyptian radio programs.

Elsewhere, elaborating on the relationship between levels 2 and 3, Badawi (1985: 19–20) writes:

> Level 2 (which corresponds to what is currently known as Modern Standard Arabic) and level 3 (which corresponds to what is known as Educated Spoken Arabic) together occupy a special position within contemporary Arab society. Although level 2 is mostly written and level 3 is mostly spoken, the relationship between them is quite different from that obtaining between level 1, which is written, and level 5, which is spoken. Levels 2 and 3 share the same interests in society, i.e. modern life and culture. The fact that one is spoken and the other is written does not put them in opposition, as it does levels 1 and 5, rather it puts them in complementary distribution. Division of labor in relation to similar interests as being in close linguistic proximity within the scheme thus holds them together; whatever is written in level 2, which covers all aspects of modern society (science, art, technology, literature, etc.) is explained and discussed in level 3 … . Levels 2 and 3, therefore, will have to be regarded, contrary to the prevailing views amongst scholars and language teachers, as merely the two sides of one coin, here termed "Modern Educated Arabic".

Meiseles's four levels

Arguing against Blanc's and Badawi's five-level classification, Meiseles (1980) proposes a four-level division "based on the fundamental fact that the existence of a mixed language variety or several such does not necessarily invalidate the dichotomous mode of the co-existence of two basic language systems … the contrast between the two systems is so consistent, that every text, or part of it, cannot help being either LA (Literary Arabic = *Fuṣḥā*) or colloquially oriented … " (Meiseles 1980: 122–3). The four levels are: Literary (or standard) Arabic, Substandard Arabic (SsA), Educated Spoken Arabic, Basic (or plain) Vernacular.

LA corresponds to both varieties of *Fuṣḥā* (i.e. heritage and contemporary) in Badawi's scheme, while basic or plain vernacular corresponds to both of Badawi's vernacular of the enlightened and vernacular of the illiterate.

Meiseles defines SsA as an Arab's attempt to speak or even write Classical Arabic (ibid.: 125). He elaborates:

> The reconstruction of the LA model is the goal, but because of a host of factors, generally extra-linguistic (spontaneity in speech or writing, insufficient knowledge of LA norms, the pressure of native dialects or a foreign

> language, speaking or writing on less formal occasions, convenience or sloppiness, etc.) many deviations from LA norms and much admixture of dialectal features occur in SsA.
>
> (Ibid.)

Recognizing that his ESA is identical to Mitchell's ESA (see below, Mitchell 1975), Meiseles defines this level of language as "the current informal language used among educated Arabs, fulfilling in general their daily language needs. It is also the main means of Arabic inter-dialectal communication, one of its most important trends being its inter-comprehensibility among speakers of different vernaculars … " (Meiseles 1980: 126).

Fuṣḥā *and* ʿĀmmiyya *with one variety in between*

In contrast to the two-way dichotomy proposed by Ferguson and the multi-level continuum of Blanc, Badawi, and Meiseles, a number of linguists have argued for the existence of only one language variety between Ferguson's H and L. This variety has been given different names by different linguists, who also disagreed as to whether it is based on *Fuṣḥā* or *ʿĀmmiyya*.

Cadora's Intercommon Spoken Arabic

According to Cadora (1965: 134) three varieties of Arabic exist side by side: Spoken Dialectal Arabic (SDA), Modern Standard Arabic (MSA) and Intercommon Spoken Arabic (ISA). He defines the latter as a "mixed spoken language … of relatively uncodified, somewhat unstable, intermediate forms" (ibid.). It is the type of spoken Arabic used by "people who have broadened their horizons through a modicum of education, travel, reading and the like [and who] do not always stick exclusively to either the commonplace dialect or the prestige standard language" (ibid.). Cadora holds that "ISA is derived essentially from a form of Arabic equivalent to the pausalized system of MSA and one or more of the dialects", while its structural system is identical to SDA (ibid.).

Bishai's Modern Inter-Arabic

Bishai (1966) discusses a different type of intermediate variety with a mixture of MSA and colloquial elements. It is the type of Arabic "used in various inter-Arab meetings which include representatives from different countries of the Arabic Middle East" (ibid.: 320).

Bishai analyzed "20 columns from the record of Arab unity debates conducted by delegations from Egypt, Syria and Iraq [which took place in 1963] as well as a short recorded speech by President Bourguiba of Tunisia [delivered in 1960]." He discovered that out of 4,000 words in the 20 columns examined, there were 188 colloquialisms representing only 26 separate items (ibid.: 321).

Five of these items appeared only once. Four of those items, repeated between two and ten times, were the following common colloquial features: *ha* + imperfect denoting futurity, *ma-sh* as negative elements, *mish* as a negative element, and *'ambi* + imperfect denoting continuous tense. The remaining 17 elements were common lexical items such as *'ēh* "what?", *imbāriḥ* "yesterday", *fih* "there is", etc. (ibid.: 321).

Bishai concludes that,

> apart from these instances of syntactic and lexical colloquial interference, the text which I examined may be said to have followed quite closely most of the morphology and syntax of "apocopated classical Arabic," i.e. Classical Arabic without its case and state endings.
>
> (Ibid.: 322)

Haddad's al-'Arabiyya al-Maḥkiyya

Haddad (1985) describes a textbook she had written which introduces the foreign learner to a type of middle Arabic, common Arabic, or third Arabic that lacks the case and mood markings and unfamiliar words of *Fuṣḥā*. It is the type of Arabic that has developed among educated Arabs in recent years. It is a living language used by professors at universities and by experts in their fields of specialization when conversing with their colleagues in different Arab countries. The lexicon of this spoken language comes from *Fuṣḥā* but includes common colloquial words that are shared by speakers from different Arab countries (Haddad 1985: 16–17).

Ibrahim's Supra-Dialectal Low

Ibrahim (1986) discusses what he describes as:

> a thriving supra-dialectal L (SDL) based on the speech of such urban centers as Cairo, Damascus, and Jerusalem … [which] has been gaining force and importance … [and] which can be compared to, say, general standard English with such major varieties as standard British, American, and Australian English.
>
> (Ibrahim 1986: 120–1)

Ryding's Formal Spoken Arabic

According to Ryding (1991: 212), Formal Spoken Arabic (FSA)

> is not the vernacular of a circumscribed geographical region, but nonetheless represents a real segment of the continuum of spoken Arabic variants – a supra-regional, prestige form of spoken Arabic practical as a means of communication throughout the Arabic-speaking world.

Ryding prefers the use of the term FSA over Educated Spoken Arabic (discussed below) but the reference of the two is the same (ibid.).

Educated Spoken Arabic

An attempt to provide a systematic study of ESA was initiated as part of a research project at the University of Leeds in the United Kingdom in the 1970s and 1980s. The project produced a number of publications whose goal was to describe its different features (Mitchell 1978, 1980, 1986; El-Hassan 1977, 1978; Sallam 1980; Mitchell and al-Hassan 1994).

Mitchell (1986: 7) describes ESA as a supra-regional standard that is created and maintained by "the interplay between written Arabic (*Fuṣḥā*) and vernacular Arabic(s)". Speakers of Arabic from different regions modify their speech in the interests of mutual intelligibility (1980: 89, 1986: 9). As El-Hassan puts it, "ESA ... draws upon both MSA and Colloquial Arabic" (El-Hassan 1978: 32). "Excluded from ESA ... are, on the one hand, stigmatized and stridently local features and forms, and, on the other, the high-flown Arabic appropriate to reading aloud, otherwise termed spoken prose" (Mitchell and al-Hassan 1994: 2). The desire for mutual intelligibility "is in large measure served by the controlling power of the written language, [while] reinforcement is provided by the substantial similarity of the grammatical base of the ... vernaculars" (Mitchell 1986: 7).

Differences between ESA, as used in Egypt and the Levant, and MSA include, among other things, differences in the morphology of verbs, passive voice formation, the presence of case markings for nouns in MSA and their absence in ESA, negation, numerals, and the dual, which is marked on nouns in ESA but on demonstratives, verbs, nouns, and adjectives in MSA (Mitchell 1986: 10–11).[1]

After reviewing the work of Blanc (1960), Badawi (1973), and Meiseles (1980), Mitchell (1986: 12–13) points out one fundamental difference between his and their view of ESA. He states:

> We do not see it as one of a series of separate varieties, on a par with MSA and the vernaculars, but rather as created and maintained by the constant interplay of written and vernacular Arabic ... educated Arabic conversation constantly oscillates between written and vernacular and written-vernacular hybridization within the scope of a sentence, phrase, or even word.

ESA is almost exclusively a spoken phenomenon. In Mitchell's words, it is "extremely difficult to find in published form examples of ESA" (1975: 78) in an environment of a "total absence of institutionalized grammars and dictionaries of ESA, in the continuing circumstances of hostility in influential circles towards its systematic study" (1980: 105). The difficulty of finding published examples of ESA may be due to the fact that it is the spoken counterpart of MSA, the accepted variety for writing by the overwhelming majority of

Arabs. As stated by Badawi (1973: 149–50), MSA represents the print form of Arabic, while ESA represents its spontaneously spoken form. So, while "the Arabic written norm (*Fuṣḥā*) is strongly institutionalized, … authoritative grammars and dictionaries of educated speech (ESA) are wholly lacking and urgently needed, according to Mitchell and al-Hassan (1994: 2).

In her PhD dissertation, Elverskog examined the morphology of verbs in ESA and concluded (Elverskog 1999: 219) that

> ESA is not simply a "patchwork" language resulting from the mixing of *Fuṣḥā* and *'Āmmiyya*, but that there are patterns and rules of grammar that ESA follows in verb formation. Although ESA is subject to considerable fluctuation in its forms of pronunciation, morphological alternations and lexical selection specific to regional dialects, the findings in the variation of the ESA verb formation of the speakers used in this study was not significant, and it has been shown that the *koineized* verb forms have striking similarities in regional dialects.

Fuṣḥā or *'Āmmiyya* base?

Linguists differ as to whether this intermediate variety (ESA, SDL, FSA, Intercommon Arabic, and Modern Inter-Arabic) has a colloquial or a *Fuṣḥā* base, but they all agree that it occupies a middle ground between the two poles and shares features of both.[2]

Ferguson (1959: 332) describes the "uncodified, unstable, intermediate forms" of Arabic, which he calls *al-lugha al-wusṭā*, as "having a highly classical vocabulary with few or no inflectional endings, with certain features of classical syntax, but with a fundamentally colloquial base in morphology and syntax".

Similarly, Blanc (1960: 92) concludes that "[d]ialectal features remain strikingly predominant in the phonology and grammar, somewhat less so in the lexicon". Badawi describes *'Āmmiyya al-muthaqqafīn* as:

> the marriage between *'Āmmiyya* and *Fuṣḥā* characteristics … between what educated speakers have mastered of *Fuṣḥā* features, which are its idioms and words and abstract forms of expression and what they have mastered of the *'Āmmiyya* features, which are its basic structure and sentence construction in general.
>
> (Badawi 1973: 151; see also Zughoul 1980: 206 and Abdulaziz 1986: 22, who make similar statements)[3]

Referring to the title of an article by T. F. Mitchell (Mitchell 1986), Wilmsen (2006: 130) gives the following brief answer to the question "What is Educated Spoken Arabic?": "[I]t is vernacular Arabic." He elaborates:

> To be sure, it is not the vernacular of muleteers and hawkers, but it is vernacular Arabic nonetheless. It exhibits much technical terminology

> drawn from formal domains but its other lexical features, along with relative and demonstrative pronouns, negation patterns, and its phonology and syntax, are largely vernacular.
>
> (Wilmsen 2006: 130)

The *Fuṣḥā-ʿĀmmiyya* continuum

While ESA seems to have dominated the discussion of the Arabic linguistic situation in the 1970s and 1980s, in the past two decades scholars have tended to describe the situation in terms of a continuum and mixed styles (Holes 2004; Mejdell 2006; Bassiouney 2006). For example, after declaring "the concept of Arabic as a 'diglossic' language … a misleading oversimplification", Holes (2004: 49) describes the behavior of most Arabic speakers as "one of constant style shifting along a cline at opposite ends of which are 'pure' MSA and the 'pure' regional dialect, more accurately conceived of as idealized constructs than real entities".

Elaborating on the complexity of this "diglossic continuum", Mejdell adds:

> The linguistic properties … – a product of the interaction of the basic varieties (*Fuṣḥā* and the colloquial) – may be correlated with dimensions of context and style – the informal-formal cline, the casual-careful cline; unplanned vs. planned discourse, and of mode/medium, i.e. spoken vs. written. The diglossic variable, i.e. those features with binary (or more) variants contrasting H and L, are potential markers of stylistic and functional differentiation and variation … .
>
> (Mejdell 2006: 4)

In an article published 37 years after the publication of the original Diglossia paper, Ferguson (1996: 59) accepts the concept of the continuum but rejects the idea of levels or discrete intermediate varieties, which would include ESA. He writes,

> I recognized the existence of intermediate forms and mentioned them briefly in the article, but I felt then and still feel that in the diglossia case the analyst finds two poles in terms of which the intermediate varieties can be described, there is no third pole.

Other aspects of the Arabic language situation

Up to this point, the focus of the discussion in this chapter has been on the relationship between *Fuṣḥā* and the colloquial varieties; not much has been said about other aspects of the Arabic sociolinguistic situation that are relevant to the main purpose of this book, namely, to present a program of teaching Arabic as a foreign language that will prepare the majority of Arabic students to function successfully in an Arabic-speaking environment. These aspects include mutual intelligibility among the Arabic colloquial varieties and a comparison with the German language situation, which is often cited as similar to that of Arabic.

Inter-dialectal intelligibility

As will be shown in Chapter 5 of this book, the issue of mutual intelligibility, or lack thereof, is of direct relevance in a discussion of teaching Arabic as a foreign language. If the colloquial varieties are mutually intelligible, then one can make the case that the foreign learner who masters one variety will be able to communicate with speakers of other mutually intelligible varieties.

Traditionally, two variables have been assumed to determine mutual intelligibility among the Arabic colloquial varieties. To quote Holes (2004: 3–4):

> The greater the distance between any two points of comparison, by and large, the greater will be the differences between the ordinary vernaculars spoken in them. It is not then surprising to find that the varieties of Arabic spoken at the extreme peripheries of the area differ from each other considerably, and certainly to the point of mutual unintelligibility if we were to compare what might be called the plain uneducated vernaculars.[4]

Systematic and comprehensive studies of mutual intelligibility among the Arabic dialects seem to be rare. The only published studies that I am aware of are two, one by Cadora (1979) and the other by Ezzat (1974). The two studies are quite limited in terms of data and scope.

Using the Swadesh List of 200 basic words, Cadora (1979, an expanded version of Cadora 1976), examined lexical compatibility among major Syro-Lebanese colloquial varieties as well as four other colloquial varieties (Baghdad-Iraq, Jidda-Saudi Arabia, Cairo-Egypt, and Casa Blanca-Morocco) in addition to Classical Arabic. Data were elicited from 18 informants, all educated native speakers representing these varieties (1979: 1–2). On the basis of an analysis of the data (ibid.: 32), Cadora concludes that "the average percentage of non-contrastive compatibility between any two given [Syro-Lebanese] varieties (except Deir ez-Zor) is approximately 96 percent". The average of "non-contrastive compatibility between the Syro-Lebanese varieties on the one hand and the other five varieties" was as shown in Table 1.1 (ibid.).

Table 1.1

	Classical Arabic	*Cairo*	*Baghdad*	*Jidda*	*Casa Blanca*
Syro-Lebanese	91%	86.2%	84.9%	80%	68%

Cadora points out that "the percentage of non-contrastive compatibility between the variants and Casa Blanca is below the 70 percent requirement for the two to be still considered varieties of the same language" (ibid.).

The role of education is emphasized in Ezzat's study (1974) of mutual intelligibility among a number of Arabic dialects. Using a recorded three-hour conversation among an Egyptian, a Jordanian, a Palestinian, a Bahraini and an Algerian and his observations as an Egyptian professor at a Lebanese university, Ezzat reaches the following conclusion about inter-dialectal mutual intelligibility (Ezzat 1974: 51). He states:

> the preceding analysis of the phonology, grammar and lexis of ESA proves that there are common linguistic features among Arabic dialects that warrant their mutual intelligibility. We have seen that an educated Egyptian like myself can understand an Algerian, a Lebanese, a Jordanian or a Bahraini. Besides, the random choice of speakers from different and mutually remote Arab countries presumably gives us a miniature of the total inter-dialectal situation among educated Arabs in the whole Arab world.

Though not designed as a study of inter-dialectal mutual intelligibility, Zughoul (1980) has demonstrated that educated speakers from different regions of the Arab world as far apart as Oman and Morocco communicate successfully, using what he describes as Educated Arabic (EA). Zughoul analyzed the speech of ten native speakers, all graduate students at the University of Texas at Austin (one Saudi, two Egyptians, one Iraqi, one Algerian, one Moroccan, one Sudanese, one Omani, and two Jordanians) who participated in a panel discussion on Arabic diglossia (ibid.: 206).

In her study of the verb morphology of ESA, in which she examined data from a variety of Arabic dialects including Egyptian, Sudanese, Lebanese, Palestinian, Omani, Yemeni, and Moroccan (Elverskog 1999: 21), Elverskog concluded "that the *koineized* verb forms have striking similarities in regional dialects".

In addition to the spread of mass education, the proliferation of satellite TV channels and movies and entertainment programs, and the movement of workers, students, tourists, and other Arabs from all over the Arab world visiting the holy places in Makka and Madina, the concept of a plain, uneducated vernacular has virtually disappeared.[5] The modern Arabic speaker, particularly the speaker who is likely to interact with speakers of other colloquial varieties, has a repertoire of tools and strategies at his/her disposal to communicate successfully with such speakers. Among these tools and strategies are the accommodation strategies employed by Maghribi (western) colloquial varieties when communicating with speakers of Mashriqi (eastern) varieties (Shiri 2002).

Is Arabic like German?

In spite of the validity of Ferguson's basic insights about the Arabic language situation, the main problem in his analysis lies in lumping the four "defining" languages in one group. Similarities of course exist between Arabic on the one hand and German, Greek, and Haitian Creole on the other, but there is a dimension to the language situation that is found in Arabic but is absent in the other three, namely the religious dimension, i.e. *Fuṣḥā* is the language of the Qur'ān and is the religious language of over one billion Muslims, including 300 million Arabic-speaking Muslims. Another major difference is that the Arabic H variety (*Fuṣḥā*) is not used for conversation by any group of speakers, while the H varieties of Haitian Creole and Swiss German are.

Mitchell (1986: 9) and Bassiouney (2009: 267) also draw comparisons between *Fuṣḥā* and High German, although they point out the basic differences.

Grouping Arabic with German or comparing Arabic diglossia to German diglossia has been particularly harmful to the cause of teaching Arabic as a foreign language since German High (understood to mean modern High German or Hochdeutsch) is often compared to *Fuṣḥā* in discussions and presentations involving Arabic pedagogy, while German Low (the various German dialects, including Swiss German) is compared to the *'Āmmiyya* varieties. An argument for introducing *Fuṣḥā* only in Arabic-as-a-foreign-language programs is generally framed in the following manner: Hochdeutsch is indisputably the variety taught to foreign learners and no reputable German-as-a-foreign-language program would contemplate offering a German dialect to the typical foreign learner, so why not treat Arabic the same way and introduce only *Fuṣḥā*?

Following is the *Encyclopedia Britannica's* definition of modern High German:

> Modern standard High German is descended from the Middle High German dialects and is spoken in the central and southern highlands of Germany, Austria, and Switzerland. It is used as the language of administration, higher education, literature, and the mass media in the Low German speech area as well.
>
> (*Encyclopedia Britannica Online*)

The key difference between *Fuṣḥā* and modern High German lies in the fact that the latter is spoken by a community of speakers while the former is not. In Ibrahim's words, a language like modern High German can be acquired "by belonging to a speech community" like those in the central and southern highlands of Germany, Austria, and Switzerland. But to which community of speakers can one belong to acquire *Fuṣḥā*? No such speech community exists.

Summary and conclusions

Based on the above literature review, a number of generalizations, of direct relevance to the main goal of the present study, can be made. But first, a word about terminology is in order.

An unfortunate development that has had an unintended adverse effect on the teaching of Arabic as a foreign language since the 1960s is the introduction and wide use of the term "Modern Standard Arabic" in the English-speaking world. This term seems to have been coined in the 1960s, as evidenced by publications using it (Abboud 1971: 17). Earlier publications seem to have used "literary" or "written" instead of "standard" (Abboud 1971: 17–19).

The spread of the term may be due to the publication of *Elementary Modern Standard Arabic* (Abboud et al. 1983, originally published in 1968), which became known in the profession as the "Orange Book". It remained the most widely used textbook in Arabic-as-a-foreign-language programs until it was displaced by *Al-Kitaab fii Taʻallum al-ʻArabiyya* (Brustad et al. 2004), first published in 1995. Offering what might be considered his definition of MSA, Abboud (1971: 3) writes:

> It is widely known that in addition to the spoken language which varies considerably from one locality to another, there exists a standard language used all over the Arab World in the press, on the radio, in the literature, and on formal occasions, commonly called Modern Standard Arabic (MSA).

One should not doubt the intentions behind introducing and using the term, but the consequences, probably unanticipated at the time, have helped spread the myth that MSA is a standard language like standard American English, standard French, or standard German. The variety of Arabic designated by this name is in fact Modern Standard *Written* Arabic.[6] It is the written counterpart of what I have called in Chapter 4 LESA and other ESA varieties. Badawi (1985: 19–20) considers the two varieties of the language (in his terminology MSA and ESA) as two sides of the same coin, one written and one spoken under the common umbrella of Modern Educated Arabic.

An American student or administrator with little or no knowledge of the Arabic sociolinguistic situation most probably would think that the situation is not different from English or French if he or she read the following statement about MSA:

> It does not seem unreasonable to expect the specialist of any persuasion to become proficient in the standard form of the language. Again, specialists in the more familiar areas of the world are expected to have proficiency in the standard language of the country or area, and it is difficult to imagine one who is proficient only in the spoken or only in the older form of the language.
>
> (Abboud 1971: 4)

Nicola (1990) and Wilmsen (2006) confirm the misleading nature of the term "Modern Standard Arabic". Nicola (1990: 42) prefers the term "modern formal Arabic" since Modern Standard Arabic "conceals the important fact that it is not the language of everyday intercourse anywhere, and hence in this sense it is far from 'standard'". Wilmsen (2006: 135, fn.) objects to the use of the term since "it fosters in novice learners the impression that they are about to acquire a form of the language that is in some sense analogous to other standard spoken language forms, for instance RP English, which it is not".[7]

Consequently, the two Arabic varieties, referred to in the literature variously as H, Classical Arabic, Modern Standard Arabic, Formal Arabic, Modern Written Arabic, and *Fuṣḥā*, on the one hand and L, colloquial Arabic, dialectal Arabic, spoken Arabic, or *'Āmmiyya*, on the other, will be referred to here for purposes of simplicity and consistency as *Fuṣḥā* and *Āmmiyya* (see Badawi 1985: 16). To the Arabic speaker, the reference of each of the two terms is clear. *Fuṣḥā* includes both MSA and Classical Arabic, the two versions of the H variety, which no one English term encompasses. H and L will be avoided because of the lower status that is likely to be associated with the L variety, although that might not have been the intention in the original usage.

The complementary roles of Fuṣḥā *and* 'Āmmiyya

Fuṣḥā and *'Āmmiyya* exist side by side and are used simultaneously, particularly by educated native speakers, each in its own general domain and for certain functions. *Fuṣḥā* is used for reading, writing, and formal, scripted (as opposed to spontaneous) speaking, while *'Āmmiyya* is used for ordinary conversation. *Fuṣḥā* is not used for ordinary conversation by any Arabic linguistic community, however small. Contrary to a widespread impression, even at formal gatherings, conversation among Arabs of different dialectal backgrounds takes place in *'Āmmiyya*, not *Fuṣḥā* (Shiri 2002: 172, Holes 2004: 6). In spite of the continuous efforts of Arabic language academies, ministries of education, and Arab radio and TV channels to impose *Fuṣḥā* for use in ordinary conversation throughout the twentieth century and the first part of the twenty-first,

> and in spite of optimism expressed by some of the new pan-Arab satellite channels as effective in spreading "good language" [i.e. *Fuṣḥā*] to the general public, there is no evidence that [it] is gaining ground as a spoken medium since [the publication of Ferguson's Diglossia paper].
>
> (Mejdell 2006: 45)

While words, phrases, and complete sentences may be borrowed freely from *Fuṣḥā*, the basic structure in terms of the morphology and syntax is that of *'Āmmiyya*. On the other hand, while it is true that the use of *'Āmmiyya* for reading and writing has increased in recent years with the availability of the internet, particularly in the form of emails, text messages, Facebook comments, and even comments on newspaper articles written in *Fuṣḥā*, the general pattern of usage still remains as described above: *Fuṣḥā* for reading, writing, and scripted speech, and *'Āmmiyya* for spontaneous conversation.

Educated native speakers of Arabic, i.e. those who master a *'Āmmiyya* variety and are educated in *Fuṣḥā*, the main medium of education throughout the Arab world, move from *Fuṣḥā* to *'Āmmiyya* and vice versa as a function of the linguistic situation or task. They read the newspaper in *Fuṣḥā* but discuss what they read in *'Āmmiyya*; a university professor reads his/her lecture notes in *Fuṣḥā* but answers questions in *'Āmmiyya*. This "style mixing" is rule-governed and is done for the most part subconsciously and effortlessly. It is an essential part of the educated speaker's linguistic competence. In Mejdell's words (see also Blanc 1960: 85),

> an educated speaker like NA2 has a range of possible 'mixed' styles at his disposal ... he can draw on the linguistic resources of Standard (*Fuṣḥā*) and EA (*'Āmmiyya*) to form various degrees of SA-oriented speech. In other words, this demonstrates that he has ... as part of his communicative competence, the ability to accommodate to more than one style level, according to some aspect of the context.
>
> (Mejdell 2006: 379)

Shared linguistic features between **Fuṣḥā** *and* **'Āmmiyya**

In spite of the presence of grammatical and lexical differences between *Fuṣḥā* on the one hand and any of the *'Āmmiyya* varieties on the other, most of the grammar and the lexicon are shared by the two. Because *Fuṣḥā* is the language of education, the more education an Arabic speaker acquires, the more shared features his/her language will exhibit.

Fuṣḥā *as a unifier*

As the language of education and most of the mass media (newspapers, radio and TV programs), *Fuṣḥā* plays an important unifying role across the Arab world. Arab children who read the same literary texts, listen to the same speeches and broadcasts, watch the same TV programs develop common linguistic repertoires, in contrast to children who lack access to the mass media and are deprived of educational opportunities.

The statement that *Fuṣḥā* is a unifying force on the Arabic linguistic scene is often coupled with the statement that the *'Āmmiyya* varieties divide the Arabs. On the one hand it is a fact that *Fuṣḥā* is virtually the same throughout the Arabic-speaking world, or from the (Persian) Gulf to the (Atlantic) Ocean, as advocates of a pan-Arab nation put it. On the other hand, not only is there Levantine, Egyptian and Moroccan Arabic, but within each of these there are sub-dialects, like Jordanian, Palestinian, Syrian, Lebanese, Cairene, Alexandrian, and Ṣa'īdī. Some would go as far as saying that every village or neighborhood has its own *'Āmmiyya* variety.

At issue here is what is meant by "*'Āmmiyya* variety". Do we mean the variety used in the village and neighborhood, or the variety used by an Egyptian professor when conversing with his Iraqi colleague at King Saud University? It is a fact that when Arabs from different regions of the Arab world converse with one another, they use their *'Āmmiyya* albeit with elements from *Fuṣḥā* and other *'Āmmiyya*s but not *Fuṣḥā* (Wilmsen 2006: 136, fn.). They use the "leveling" and "classicizing" techniques referred to above to ensure successful communication. While they may borrow words and expressions from *Fuṣḥā*, they negate their sentences with *mish* (*mush or mū*), not *laysa*; they ask their questions with *ēsh*, *shū*, *ēh*, but not *mādha*; they use *rāḥ*, not *ðahaba* and *shāf* in place of *ra'ā*; and there is a complete absence of the case and mood system, the one feature that clearly sets *Fuṣḥā* apart from the spoken Arabic dialects. This is what takes place when the Egyptian and Iraqi professors converse.

Such a process is natural, and it takes place in all natural languages, where the language of education enriches a speaker's native dialect and where speakers of different varieties of the same language accommodate one another to facilitate communication without necessarily abandoning their own variety of speech.

One could make the case then that the colloquial base, shared by the various Arabic *'Āmmiyya*s, enriched by *Fuṣḥā* words and expressions, and not *Fuṣḥā exclusively*, unifies the Arabs linguistically at the practical, conversational level.[8]

Mutual intelligibility among the 'Āmmiyya *varieties*

The *'Āmmiyya* varieties are mutually intelligible. Mutual intelligibility is possible because the bulk of vocabulary and grammatical structures are shared among them. In general, and as was pointed out above, the percentage of shared features increases with education, geographical proximity, exposure to the mass media and entertainment outlets, and interaction with speakers of other varieties. According to Ibrahim (1986: 121), ESA varieties in particular have wide comprehensibility beyond the geographical areas in which they are actually spoken. This is particularly true of Egyptian and Levantine. It should be noted here that speakers of different *'Āmmiyya* varieties do not necessarily abandon their varieties and adopt the varieties of those with whom they communicate; they simply employ elements at their disposal from *Fuṣḥā* and other colloquial varieties to ensure successful communication.

Disagreement over intermediate varieties[9]

The above discussion shows widely divergent views on intermediate varieties between the two "poles" of *Fuṣḥā* on one side and *'Āmmiyya* on the other. The views range from one such variety (ESA) to an unlimited number of varieties where

> the linguistic range between the poles [constitutes] an uncharted sea of intermediate shades, whose overall picture is one of a state of flux; or … an open language system which has theoretically, every shade of a finite, but huge number of varieties, ranging from plain local vernaculars to the standard descriptive non-native LA (literary Arabic, i.e. *Fuṣḥā*).
>
> (Meiseles 1980: 120)

Prestige

Prestige was listed by Ferguson as one of the phenomena that distinguish diglossic language situations from standard-with-dialects situations, and in the case of Arabic *Fuṣḥā* is the prestigious variety (see above). A number of studies that have appeared since the publication of Ferguson's article argue (1) that the situation in Arabic is not as simple as that and (2) that the colloquial varieties have their own "pecking order of prestige" (Mitchell 1986: 9; see also Hussein and El-Ali 1989).

For historical, political, and religious reasons, *Fuṣḥā* enjoys a level of prestige that is unmatched by *'Āmmiyya*, which is generally stigmatized by the overwhelming majority of Arabs and often considered corrupt and divisive.[10] *Fuṣḥā* is the language of education, most written literature and high culture, and is a symbol of Arab unity and a glorious past (Abd-el-Jawad 1986: 58). It is also the language of the Qur'ān and the studies associated with it. This "pan-Arab" prestige of *Fuṣḥā* gives way at the practical level to certain urban dialects, particularly the dialects of capital cities (Ibrahim 1986), where speakers of non-urban, less prestigious varieties adapt their speech to that of urban centers. In Mitchell's words, the *'Āmmiyya* "of a given region … has its own pecking order of prestige, especially between urban and rural" (Mitchell 1986: 9).

Notes

1 On ESA features, see further Zughoul 1980: 206 and Elverskog 1999, particularly chapters IV–IX.

2 On ESA as an independent entity and not merely a "patchwork language resulting from the mixing of *Fuṣḥā* and *'Āmmiyya*", see further Elverskog 1999: 219.

3 The reader may recall Bishai's account of Modern Inter-Arabic, discussed earlier in the chapter, where he concludes that the text he "examined may be said to have followed quite closely most of the morphology and syntax of 'apocopated classical Arabic,' i.e. classical Arabic (*Fuṣḥā*) without its case and state endings" (Bishai 1966: 322). This conclusion contradicts those of Ferguson, Blanc, and Badawi, but one has to take the following into account: First, that Bishai's texts cannot be described as ordinary conversations among native speakers; they are political negotiations and a political speech. Second, the case and mood system (*'I'rāb*) is the major grammatical feature that clearly sets *Fuṣḥā* apart from *'Āmmiyya*. Its absence and the presence of a number of features that clearly belong to *'Āmmiyya* (negation and imperfect marking, the use of the demonstrative pronoun in reverse order to *Fuṣḥā*) cast serious doubt on the validity of Bishai's conclusion.

4 Bassiouney (2009: 21–6) seems to underestimate the importance of mutual intelligibility as a critical factor in distinguishing dialects of the same language from distinct languages. She gives a theoretical example of three sentences where she compares five Arabic dialects (Tunisian, Egyptian, Lebanese, Iraqi, and Saudi) which represent what she considers to be the five major dialect groups. Using the same example, she then shows the differences between the two Germanic languages German and Dutch and concludes that "the differences [between German and Dutch] are similar to the differences between the different vernaculars examined above". She adds: "The examples make one wonder about differences between

different languages and different varieties and whether terms like 'language' and 'variety' are not political terms rather than linguistic ones" (ibid.: 26). I think the real issue here is mutual intelligibility. While I am not sure about the mutual intelligibility between Tunisian and the other four varieties, no one would question the mutual intelligibility of the other four. Are German and Dutch mutually intelligible? If yes, then linguistically they should be considered dialects of the same language.

5 This is termed by Abd-el-Jawad a process of standardization which is fostered by "The spread of education, mass media, the development of the means of communication, social and geographic mobility … " (Abd-el-Jawad 1986: 57).

6 Abd-el-Jawad (1987: 359) uses the term "Written Modern Standard Arabic".

7 Zughoul (1980: 207) points out that "The concept of MSA is unheard of in the Arab World".

8 One may go as far as to say that in reality the Arabs are united in their hostility to certain features of *Fuṣḥā*, such as the system of *'i'raab.*

9 Kaye (1972: 37) lumps mixtures of MSA and the colloquial such as "Inter-Arabic, Intercommon Spoken Arabic, Spoken Classical Arabic, Middle Arabic … and Spoken Literary Arabic" with MSA and considers both the MSA system and the mixture as "ill-defined systems" to be contrasted with the well-defined systems of the colloquials.

10 This stigmatization is reinforced at various levels in the Arabic-speaking world. Not only is *Fuṣḥā* the official language of all Arab countries, but, according to Cachia (1967: 20), "works in the colloquial receive no recognition from the Egyptian Academy, and do not qualify for State prizes". Al-Khūlī (1987: 91–2) writes: " … most writers feel that the language of conversation and living (*'Āmmiyya*) … is like filth (*rijs*) that should be avoided and a disease from which to seek protection." The stigmatization of *'Āmmiyya* seems to have found its way to Arabic programs in the United States. Wilmsen (2006: 137, fn.) writes: "At both universities where I studied, language requirement credit was not granted to students who for some reason or another studied a[n Arabic] dialect."

2 Changing Student Goals

The early days of Arabic study

The study of Arabic as a foreign language dates back to the early days of Islam when new converts, whose language was not Arabic, sought to understand the language of their sacred text, the Qur'ān. This may explain the fact that the early Arabic grammarians, such as Sībawayh, were of non-Arab origin.

Interest in the study of Arabic in the Western world goes back to at least the end of the sixteenth century. Arabic was studied for the "wisdom" of the Arabs and to read works written in Arabic in such disciplines as mathematics and astronomy (Versteegh 2006: 7). Most of the early Arabists did not have contacts with the Arabic-speaking world; "[T]hey were interested in the Classical language, and in most cases, did not even know about the existence of a colloquial language" (ibid.).

In the United States Arabic was introduced at Harvard in the seventeenth century (McCarus 1992: 207) following Hebrew, Chaldaic, and Syriac. It was introduced at Yale in 1700, Dartmouth and Andover in 1807, and Princeton 1822 (ibid.). In all these institutions, the interest in Arabic was part of a larger interest in Semitic languages because of their relevance in the study of the Bible (Abboud 1971: 1; Allen 1992: 227).

By the end of the nineteenth century Arabic was offered at 16 major departments of semitics (McCarus 1992: 208).

American participation in World War II demonstrated an urgent need for Americans with a sound command of Arabic, which motivated the US government to fund different programs for training in the language, both *Fuṣḥā* and the colloquial dialects (Abboud 1971: 2). The Arabic programs at the Foreign Service Institute and Defense Language Institute in which *Fuṣḥā* and a number of dialects are taught are continuations of these early efforts (McCarus 1992: 209). The goals of these programs were tied to national security interests, such as military intelligence and working for US missions and aid organizations in Arab countries.

Modern Standard Arabic and the "Orange Books"

In a significant departure from the standard practice at academic institutions of focusing on the study of Classical (medieval) Arabic texts, it was unanimously agreed by the participants in a workshop held at Columbia University in 1966 "that it is practically and methodically sound for all students of Arabic to begin their training with modern *Fuṣḥā*, which became known as Modern Standard Arabic (MSA) and then, if desired, to undertake medieval Arabic at the advanced level" (ibid.: 212).

In an article on Arabic language instruction in the United States, Abboud (1971) discusses the types of students who were studying Arabic at American colleges and universities at the time of its publication. He states that there were two main types: First, graduate students who had made a commitment to some field of Middle Eastern studies. These students consisted of a number of sub-groups according to their interests, with some interested in learning a colloquial variety to do field work, others who needed a reading knowledge of MSA to read modern printed materials, and a third sub-group who were interested in medieval manuscripts.

The second group, according to Abboud, "are mainly undergraduates, many of whom have no definite commitment to the field but take Arabic to fulfill foreign language requirements … ".

A set of books, which became known as the "Orange Books", were written with the goal of introducing MSA to the foreign learner and using it for all language skills, including conversation. These books dominated the field of Arabic instruction for over twenty years until the appearance of the *al-Kitāb* series in the mid-1990s.

Although dialect courses were offered along with MSA, the latter remained the focus (Allen 1992: 230). The establishment of the Arabic Summer School at Middlebury College in 1983 ushered in a new era for MSA, which was the only variety introduced at the School. MSA was made to function in situations where colloquial is normally used in Arab society (McCarus 1992: 216). In Allen's words (1992: 231), "it was decided by the director in conjunction with heads of the Arabic programs at the universities involved, that the language of instruction would be MSA *in all four skills*" (emphasis in the original).

A similar shift from old *Fuṣḥā* (Classical Arabic) to the new version of *Fuṣḥā* (MSA) and the introduction of colloquial Arabic in the classroom also took place in Europe in the second half of the twentieth century (Versteegh 2006: 9), for different reasons. The introduction of colloquial Arabic was the result of the existence of large numbers of Arab immigrant children in European schools and universities. According to Versteegh (ibid.: 10), "The new students' familiarity with spoken Arabic brought home the fact that teaching the standard language (MSA) was only part of the story."

Arabic instruction in Europe followed the same pattern that was followed in the United States: "the usual choice was to start with MSA and then introduce a dialect, usually Egyptian because of its wide distribution in the Arab world" (ibid.). This has become the standard practice in the overwhelming majority of Arabic-as-a-foreign-language programs everywhere.

The proficiency movement: new student needs

MSA was the obvious choice in most programs because it offered a practical solution to the thorny issue of which colloquial variety to introduce in the classroom: No single variety is accepted in the Arabic-speaking world as the standard spoken one and there is no clear way of deciding which variety would be the most useful for the learner.

Two developments challenged this way of thinking. The first was the rise of the proficiency movement, which focused on the development of measurable skills for real communication in language and took the educated native speaker as the model of instruction to achieve proficiency. The second development was the rise in the number of students interested in learning Arabic, with many of them interested in traveling to the Arab world and speaking with Arabs.

The results of a survey of over 500 students from 24 American and Canadian universities, published by Kirk Belnap in 1987, clearly show that a majority of respondents listed literature and culture (56.3 percent), traveling/living in the Middle East (57 percent), and talking to Arabs (51.1 percent) as the three most important factors for studying Arabic. Other factors listed were: research (34.9 percent), love of languages (44.7 percent), reading the Qur'ān/religious texts (29.8 percent), general education requirement (25.4 percent), having Arab friends (25.4 percent), for fun (23.4 percent), preparing for a career (19.9 percent), heritage (14.4 percent), and linguistic research (7 percent) (Belnap 1987: 33).

A similar survey by Belnap (2006) confirms these earlier findings. Of 12 items listed as reasons for taking Arabic, the five chosen most often were: interacting with Arabic speakers (88.4 percent), traveling to the Arab world (78.6 percent), reading the modern Arabic press (67.5 percent), understanding Arab culture (67 percent), understanding TV and radio broadcasts (66 percent).

Husseinali (2006) investigated the initial motivation of 120 learners of Arabic as a foreign language (AFL) who were enrolled in first- and second-year Arabic classes at a major American university. Among the 16 items eliciting information about participants' reasons for studying AFL, the two reasons chosen by the highest number of participants (90.8 percent and 90 percent, respectively) were to "converse with people" and "travel to Arab countries" (400–1).

A fourth study by Palmer (2007: 116) shows that 88 percent of 650 Arabic students surveyed indicated that they either agree (19.1 percent) or strongly agree (68.7 percent) with the following statement: "Studying Arabic is important because it will allow me to interact with people who speak it." This, according to Palmer, shows that the vast majority of the students are learning Arabic to communicate with native speakers.

Learning to communicate with native speakers means learning to speak a *ʿĀmmiyya* variety since that is what native speakers use to communicate. A study by Shiri (2013: 574) of student attitudes in Arabic study-abroad programs shows a significant change towards the importance of learning a *ʿĀmmiyya* variety as a result of their study-abroad experience: the percentage of students who believed that "learning a dialect was extremely important" went up from 59 percent before to 88 percent after attending the Arabic program abroad.

The above studies show that the goals of Arabic students now differ significantly from those of earlier generations who studied the language for the "wisdom" of the Arabs, to read Arabic writings on science and philosophy, or even to read Arabic literature and study the structure of the language. The primary objective of the new generation of students is to use the language the way they would use any other modern living language: communicate with its speakers, visit Arabic-speaking countries, and read and write what Arabs read and write. In other words, they are interested in overall proficiency in the language, i.e. mastering all skills necessary for this proficiency: listening, speaking, reading, and writing.

Considering the diglossic language situation in the Arabic-speaking world and taking the "educated native speaker" as the model for the Arabic foreign learner, proficiency in the four language skills translates into the following (see Ferguson 1971; Allen 1989; Heath 1990; Younes 1990; 1995a, 2006; Alosh 1991, 1992; Al-Batal 1992):

1 mastering the skill of listening in both *Fuṣḥā* and *ʿĀmmiyya*. For example, ordinary conversation is conducted in *ʿĀmmiyya*, while news broadcasts are conducted in *Fuṣḥā*. Certain functions may involve a mixture of the two, such as interviews, political speeches, and religious sermons;
2 mastering the skill of speaking in *ʿĀmmiyya* for use in ordinary conversation. For students at advanced levels, mastering the skill of speaking in *Fuṣḥā* may become necessary for delivering speeches or for formal interviews;
3 mastering the skill of reading in *Fuṣḥā*;
4 mastering the skill of writing in *Fuṣḥā*.

No less important than these four skills is the skill to navigate successfully between the two language varieties according to the situation and linguistic function.

In the next chapter I will discuss how the Arabic teaching profession has met, or failed to meet, the changing needs of Arabic students.

3 Responding to the Needs of the Modern AFL Learner

Fuṣḥā only or primarily

Over forty years ago, Abboud (1971: 4) wrote:

> [Arabic programs] now begin with MSA and only later, if at all, offer a colloquial. This is mainly because MSA is more useful for the average student, since after gaining some competence in it, he can remain culturally informed and can maintain his proficiency by using newspapers, magazines, books, broadcasts, etc., which are available in the libraries of many institutions. This would be impossible for the colloquial; the student would have to live in the Arab World in order to use it, as very few will have the chance to do.

The pattern of introducing *Fuṣḥa* first and *ʿĀmmiyya* later, if at all, became and still remains the dominant one in AFL programs (Ryding 1991: 212; Wilmsen 2006: 125; Palmer 2007: 118; Abdalla and Al-Batal 2011–12: 16; Shiri 2013: 570) in spite of the drastically different needs of Arabic students and in spite of the repeated calls for different approaches to teaching Arabic (Nicola 1990; Younes 1990, 1995a, 2006; Al-Batal 1992; Wilmsen 2006, among others). I believe that there are a number of reasons – some practical, some historical, others ideological – that have contributed to the persistence of this pattern. Unless these reasons are understood and dealt with, the pattern is likely to persist and the needs of the new generations of Arabic students will not be met in a satisfactory manner.

Reasons for privileging *Fuṣḥā*

The ideological and historical reasons for privileging *Fuṣḥā* include the prestige it enjoys among Arabs and Muslims because it is the language of Islam and its holy book, the Qur'ān. It is associated with a rich Arab/Muslim history and cultural heritage and with the dream of Arab unity. It is the official language of all Arabic-speaking countries and is often listed as such in the constitutions of Arab countries (Bassiouney 2009: 119), together with Islam as the state religion. (See Zughoul 1980: 203–4 and references cited there.) It is also the language of education and high culture. *ʿĀmmiyya*, by contrast, is generally viewed negatively: it is divisive, a Western conspiracy against *Fuṣḥā*; it represents the weaknesses of the present, associated with poverty and ignorance; it is a disease to be treated. For example, the best-known Arabic novelist and Nobel Laureate of the twentieth century, Naguib Mahfouz, described *ʿĀmmiyya*, which he strictly avoided in his writings, as a disease (Dawwārah 1996: 368, Cachia 1967: 20). Sa'īd (1964: c–d) claims that the study of *ʿĀmmiyya* has been promoted in the West as a conspiracy to marginalize or replace *Fuṣḥa*. In the words of al-Badrāwi Zahrān (1989: 89): "*ʿĀmmiyya* has an injurious influence on *Fuṣḥā* … a really disturbing problem … the danger of *ʿĀmmiyyāt* (plural of *Āmmiyya*) is not restricted to one Arab community but includes all speakers of Arabic."[1]

Suspicions about a conspiracy for strengthening *Āmmiyya* and weakening *Fuṣḥā* may have been well founded. According to Bassiouney (2009: 237),

> The British aimed at weakening SA (Standard Arabic, i.e. *Fuṣḥā*) [in Egypt] by promoting the vernacular (*Āmmiyya*) … [they] tried hard to raise the status of the colloquial at the expense of SA. They believed that children should learn the language they speak … .

Bassiouney adds:

> [the British] elevated the status of ECA (Egyptian Colloquial Arabic) rather than SA by emphasizing the distinctiveness of the Egyptian identity as opposed to the Arabic identity. They were aiming to eradicate any Egyptian national aspirations and to tighten their grip on Egypt.
>
> (Ibid.: 237)

While *Fuṣḥā* is promoted at the official level, particularly by the Arab language academies and ministries of education, *ʿĀmmiyya* is generally marginalized and resisted. According to Sawaie (2006), one of the 2001 goals of the Arabic Language Academy in Damascus, which was founded in 1919, was "finding ways to limit the spread of dialects in all spheres of language use".

The "conspiracy" against *Fuṣḥa* and the promotion of *ʿĀmmiyya* at its expense, regardless of one's position on the issue, still influence the way many Arabs, including Arabic teachers, view the two varieties of the language. This has the direct result of privileging *Fuṣḥa* at the expense of *ʿĀmmiyya* in many Arabic programs.[2]

Among the practical reasons for the exclusive introduction of *Fuṣḥa* in the Arabic classroom, one can list the following: First, the fact that there is only one *Fuṣḥa* but many *ʿĀmmiyya* varieties, so if one needs to introduce a *ʿĀmmiyya* variety, it is difficult or impossible because there are so many. "[T]his dilemma was mostly addressed or, some would argue, avoided by teaching MSA alone and counting on students to 'pick up' the dialects if they went abroad" (Shiri 2013: 566).

Second, since *Fuṣḥā* is the language of education and writing of all kinds, instructional materials, particularly written materials, are much more readily available in *Fuṣḥā* than in the *ʿĀmmiyya* varieties.

Third, as the living language of the Arabs, *ʿĀmmiyya* is in a constant state of change, particularly since the middle of the twentieth century as a result of political and economic developments and the spread of education in the Arab world. Such drastic change, combined with the fact that *ʿĀmmiyya* is not permitted to compete with *Fuṣḥā* as a written medium (refer to the section "Writing LESA" in Chapter 4), makes it seem unstable, highly variable, and not subject to codification (Badawi 1985: 20). While such variation is the norm in language (Ryding 1991: 213), one can see the difficulty of having to provide grammars and develop instructional materials in *ʿĀmmiyya* when materials are readily available in a related and stable form of the language.

Fourth, for many Arabic teachers, particularly those who studied Arabic as a first language, learning and teaching Arabic means learning to read and write *Fuṣḥā* and studying its grammar. Since they have already mastered a *ʿĀmmiyya* variety by the time they start school, the idea of learning *ʿĀmmiyya* in a school setting is foreign to them.

Consequences of privileging *Fuṣḥā*

This privileging of *Fuṣḥā* may have been sufficient for students studying the "wisdom" of the Arabs and Muslims of the Golden Age of Islam, but it does not prepare the majority of the new generations of Arabic students whose goal is to learn Arabic in order to speak to Arabs or travel to the Arab world, as we saw in Chapter 2. Imagine the shock and frustration of a student who has studied Arabic for two or three years, mastered the grammar of *Fuṣḥā* and is able to read classical Arabic literary works, who then travels to an Arab country and cannot communicate with native speakers about basic needs.[3] Or imagine the reaction of the student who had spent hours trying to master the dozen shapes of *laysa* (not) and finds out upon visiting an Arab country that no Arabic speaker in fact uses any of these shapes in conversation but simply the word *mish*.

A comment by a student who went on a study abroad is revealing in this respect. He/she writes:

> Before the program, I was stupid. I thought I could walk around the Arab world speaking MSA and be just fine, and maybe that's technically true, but the quality of interaction increases so much once you have a foundation in *ʿĀmmiyya*. I laugh at my pre-program self.
>
> (Quoted in Shiri 2013: 574)

Probably worse than the feeling that one has learned the wrong variety of the language and thus is unable to converse with native speakers is the feeling of humiliation experienced by some students who try to converse with Arabic speakers in *Fuṣḥā*. In Palmer's words, "It is also not uncommon for native

Arabs to snicker at foreigners who only speak the formal language (*Fuṣḥā*), thus potentially causing a sense of humiliation" (Palmer 2007: 112).[4]

Another student in Shiri's study writes: "You can only understand news and readings [with MSA = *Fuṣḥā*]. But for actual communication, MSA is pretty useless and people think you sound like a fool."

There are of course occasions when an Arabic speaker can and is willing to carry out a conversation in MSA, but such a conversation is bound to be brief and would only amount to a performance, not real communication. Reflecting on his experience while in a study-abroad program in Jordan, an American student captures this phenomenon well. He writes,

> We came here and started speaking *Fuṣḥā* to taxi drivers, restaurant owners, etc. Some knew *Fuṣḥā* and were able to speak to us, but many didn't. We were laughed at, not understood and stood out as foreigners. Then, when I began to pick up and use the dialect, reactions changed immediately; I was taken more seriously. I was complimented on my Arabic, and I was asked if I was Jordanian, and I was able to hold lengthy conversations with people. The doors that can open for you if you use the dialect (or at least attempt to use it) are unlimited.

The exclusive introduction of *Fuṣḥā* or introducing it first and teaching students to communicate in it about daily functions, has resulted in what Karin Ryding (2006: 16) refers to as "Reverse Privileging", which she posits as the "key issue facing teaching Arabic as a foreign language in America today". She states:

> This reverse privileging is a central reason why the Arabic field faces complex issues in defining proficiency skill levels and how to assess them, and why Arabic students still may get discouraged early on in their coursework because they lack the tools of primary discourse that would allow them to begin to interact with Arab peers and friends on an informal level. It also constitutes one reason for the extraordinary low number of Arabic speakers at the superior and distinguished levels in America today, because the gap in communicative competence at the lower levels undermines the ultimate achievement of communicative competence and confidence at the higher levels. What other foreign language educators take for granted as foundational skills of interactional facility in the target language, academic Arabic programs often postpone or minimize. This is analogous to building a major edifice without a deep and fortified foundation. The more advanced a student becomes in literary or theoretical Arabic studies, the more he or she experiences a disjuncture between his or her classroom achievement and the lack of ability to deal with the most basic quotidian matters.

When students are taught to discuss everyday issues, such as self-identification, family, work, school, and the weather in *Fuṣḥā*, which is not used by native speakers for such functions, they are deprived of the opportunity to converse with these speakers in a meaningful communicative manner and are shut out of any opportunities of reinforcement, which is essential to the development of language proficiency. As Williams (1990: 46) argues, this situation (introducing *Fuṣḥā* before *'Āmmiyya*) will "deprive students of the many benefits of oral reinforcement, which early introduction of CO [*'Āmmiyya*] can give". Oral reinforcement in MSA "is bound to be artificial" (ibid). Consequently, graduates of an Arabic program using this approach may leave it with little or no ability to converse or understand ordinary conversation.[5]

One may state in summary that the Arabic teaching profession has for the most part not taken into consideration the needs of the typical Arabic-as-a-foreign-language student. As Wilmsen writes (2006: 136, fn.), based on personal experience as an Arabic student:

> At one of the universities in which I studied, the practice of the department was to administer a questionnaire to students to assess their needs and goals in studying Arabic … the bulk of students claimed that they wanted to learn to speak Arabic. Regardless of their expressed wishes, the same syllabus was implemented every year, heavy on grammar and reading, light on any sort of speaking … .

Such "stubbornness" and disregard for students on the part of the syllabus designers is very likely to be a reflection or a result of one or more of the reasons cited above for the privileging of *Fuṣḥā* at the expense of *'Āmmiyya*.

Notes

1 For more statements by leading Arab intellectuals of the twentieth century denouncing *Āmmiyya*, see Zughoul (1980: 205–6).

2 The perceived conspiracy against *Fuṣḥa* might be one dimension of the myths and prejudices that Abboud (1971) mentions when he comments: "Native speakers [teaching Arabic at American colleges and Universities] on the whole are not too quick to adjust to the facts of American education or to abandon their myths and prejudices about the Arabic language."

3 In Parkinson's words (Parkinson 1985: 11): "[T]hey (students who developed some speaking ability in MSA) have no trouble telling you about the visit of the foreign minister of Morocco to Libya, but when it comes to reserving a hotel room, or buying a train ticket or a sack of oranges they are totally lost." Parkinson adds (ibid.: 26) "what is the point of learning to ask directions of a policeman, when we know from experience that if a student did ask directions of a policeman in Standard Arabic (MSA) either the policeman would not understand the question or the student would not understand the answer?"

4 Abd-el-Jawad (1987: 360), commenting on native speaker behavior, writes: "Using MSA consistently in speaking to others would be a source of ridicule and unpleasant outcome."

5 One of the results of the focus on *Fuṣḥā* and using it for conversation is the development in the students of a fear of speaking. In Wilmsen's words (2006: 130): "By the end of … two painful years of awkward dialogues [in *Fuṣḥā*] … we students had all inherited the classical grammarians' horror of errors and were afraid to open our mouths."

4 Integration

A successful AFL program is one that meets the needs of as many of its students as possible. And since, as was shown in Chapter 2, the majority of these students embark on the study of Arabic with the goal of understanding, speaking, reading, and writing the language, then such a program would introduce *Fuṣḥā* and a *ʿĀmmiyya* variety and treat the two as equally important, with each fulfilling a certain set of functions and without privileging one over the other. Teaching only *Fuṣḥā* or only *ʿĀmmiyya* or the two in two separate tracks will result in privileging one over the other and create an artificial division between the two varieties that does not exist in the real world and will deprive the learner of the opportunity to develop the skill to use the two varieties in a complementary manner, as native speakers do. I will argue in this chapter that the only type of program that avoids this privileging and that most effectively prepares the AFL learner to deal with the realities of the Arabic sociolinguistic situation is what I call an "integrated program".

What is "integration"?

Integrating *Fuṣḥā* and *ʿĀmmiyya* is not a new concept. Abboud (1971: 4) mentions integration as an alternative approach to teaching only *Fuṣḥā*. He states: "An alternate solution to the problem of which form of Arabic to teach may lie in an approach where the colloquial and MSA are integrated into one course. This has been tried, with success, in the Defense Language Institute." It seems that the practice was later abandoned.

Although Nicola (1990) does not explicitly mention the word "integrated", the method he advocates involves integrating the two varieties, albeit not from the beginning of Arabic instruction. He writes (Nicola 1990: 42) that there are pedagogical, practical, linguistic, and cultural justifications to "start with Educated Spoken Arabic (ESA), then proceed with the written language while using ESA for speaking all the time". Nicola's approach draws "mainly … on the natural approach" to foreign language instruction advocated by Terrell and Krashen in the 1970s and 1980s, which "is designed after the manner a child learns his native language" (ibid.).

After briefly presenting the different approaches to Arabic language instruction (the Classical Arabic approach, the MSA approach, the colloquial approach, the middle language approach, and the simultaneous approach), Al-Batal (1992: 298–302) makes the following proposal:

> a modification of the simultaneous approach … [a] basic feature of the proposed approach is that it should reflect in the classroom the diglossic situation … as it exists in the Arab world today. It should introduce MSA as a variety that is mainly written but that is also spoken in a multitude of situations. It should also introduce an Arabic dialect as a variety that is used mainly for daily life communications but also as a vehicle for forms of literary expression.
>
> (Ibid.: 298)

Al-Batal (ibid.) adds, "The proposed approach does not treat these varieties of Arabic [*Fuṣḥā* and *'Āmmiyya*] as discrete and separate entities … but as components of one integrated linguistic system."

Wilmsen (2006: 134) advocates an Arabic program in which "the default should be to begin with the vernacular, ideally two full years, with the instruction in the formal written code (*Fuṣḥā*) beginning to be worked into the curriculum at the start of the second year".[1]

In Younes (1990) I advocated the Integrated Approach and in the same year I started building an integrated program at Cornell University. Also in the same year I began work on a set of instructional materials following the integrated philosophy, which resulted in the publication of two textbooks (Younes 1995b and 1999). In Cornell's integrated Arabic Program, now in its twenty-fourth year, all instruction and instructional materials follow the integrated philosophy. The rest of this chapter will be devoted to a detailed account of integration: its philosophy and its implementation in the classroom and in instructional materials as well as a response to the objections typically raised against it.

Integration: rationale and basic description

The underlying philosophy of the Integrated Approach (IA) to Arabic language instruction is the desire to reflect in the Arabic classroom and in all Arabic instructional materials the manner in which Arabic is used in real life by native speakers (see Younes 1990: 106; Al-Batal 1992: 298). This means that conversation and discussion in the classroom and in the instructional materials take place in *'Āmmiyya*, while reading and writing activities take place in *Fuṣḥā*. As mentioned in the previous chapter, the two varieties of the language play complementary and equally important roles (Younes 2006: 159, Shiri 2013: 575). The three-volume textbook series *'Arabiyyat al-Naas*, which I have co-authored and which has recently been re-published, follows the IA. Every unit in each of the three books includes materials and activities that involve both varieties of the language. Written materials are introduced in *Fuṣḥā*, while some listening materials are presented in *Fuṣḥā* and other materials in *'Āmmiyya*, depending on the theme and the nature of the materials themselves. Students read texts written in *Fuṣḥā* but discuss them in *'Āmmiyya*. The key word here is "integration" or "complementarity". It is not random mixing (*khalṭ* or *mazj*). *Fuṣḥā* and *'Āmmiyya* do not replace one another, come one after the other, or duplicate each other. They complement one another. Each variety is used in its proper context and for the functions it is actually used for by native speakers in real communication. Each has its own role and the two roles are intertwined.

The IA was started at Cornell University in the fall semester of 1990. It is my belief that it is the only sound, logical, and practical approach to introducing Arabic to the foreign learner.[2]

The main goal of the program is to prepare students for real proficiency in Arabic right from the beginning, including the sociolinguistic skill of using each variety of the language in its proper context. The program introduces spoken Levantine Arabic as the *'Āmmiyya* variety. (More will be said on which dialect to choose for the Arabic program in Chapter 5.) Emphasis in the first few hours of instruction is on the familiar, concrete, and informal, for which *'Āmmiyya* is particularly appropriate. Reading and writing activities, in which *Fuṣḥā* is used, are also introduced in the first few hours, building on areas of overlap between the two language varieties, such as numbers, geography of the Arab world, days of the week, and material presented in tabular form. Such materials do not require the use of features found in one of the varieties but not in the other, such as the case and mood system (*I'rāb*). *Fuṣḥā* occupies an increasingly prominent role in the curriculum with the move towards the less concrete and more formal, but integration remains an important feature of the program. An attempt is made to develop the four language skills simultaneously, in addition to the ability to move from one Arabic variety to another. Throughout the course, speaking activities are conducted in *'Āmmiyya*, while reading and writing are conducted in *Fuṣḥā*. Typically, each lesson involves work on more than one language skill, which results in a continuous and spontaneous movement from *Fuṣḥā* to *'Āmmiyya* and vice versa as a function of the linguistic situation that is being replicated and the language material used in this replication. Following common practice by native speakers, material presented in *Fuṣḥā* is discussed in *'Āmmiyya*, which contributes to the continuous movement between the two language varieties and gives students the opportunity to develop this important skill.

Implementation

Following is an example of an integrated unit taken from the first part of the textbook series (*'Arabiyyat al-Naas Part I*), which consists of 21 units. Unit 10, whose theme is school and education (الدراسة), has five lessons. The first lesson includes two short video clips in which Emily, an American student studying in Jordan, and her Jordanian roommate Fadwā have a conversation about courses and Jordanian and American universities. The conversation takes place in colloquial Levantine, referred to here as Levantine Educated Spoken Arabic (LESA). The main part of the second lesson is a reading text about ancient Arab universities (*al-Azhar, al-Zaytūna, al-Qarawiyyīn*). The third lesson also consists of a reading text (a written diary): Emily writes about the importance of the *Tawjīhi* exam in Jordan. The fourth lesson focuses on the grammar points introduced in the listening (video) and reading materials of the unit, and includes activities and exercises to help students master them (the difference between *min 'ahamm* and *'ahamm min*, the different uses of *mā*, verb-subject (dis-)agreement, relative pronouns, and a sociolinguistic corner in which some of the lexical and grammatical differences between *Fuṣḥā* and the LESA, found in this unit, are discussed). The fifth and final lesson includes wrap-up activities: a simple song about study, vocabulary-building exercises (matching opposites, plurals, a crossword puzzle) and a final speaking/writing activity that ties the different elements of the theme together. For this final activity students are asked to choose one of two topics and:

1. create a dialogue with another student in which they discuss their reasons for choosing the school they are attending, then write it up in about fifty words;
2. study the history of their university or college (or any other university they choose), prepare a short outline and present it to the class, then write it up in about fifty words.

Aside from the grammar explanations, which, at this stage, are presented in English and which are meant for students to read on their own, the general principle in the presentation of the material in the unit is that conversation and discussion take place in *'Āmmiyya* and reading and writing take place in *Fuṣḥā*.

The *'Āmmiyya* component

For the *'Āmmiyya* component of the program, Levantine Arabic, more specifically what is described below as Levantine ESA (LESA for short) has been chosen. The reasons for choosing this variety are discussed in detail in Chapter 5 under "Which dialect?". In this chapter a description of LESA as used in our integrated program is provided.

What is Levantine Educated Spoken Arabic (LESA)?

A main characteristic of this variety, and of standard varieties in general, is the spontaneous suppression of regionalized features and forms that are not likely to be understood by speakers of other varieties, and the inclusion of more "standard" forms.[3]

For a representative sample of LESA materials the reader is referred to the 'Arabiyyat al-Naas textbook series in which all conversation and most listening passages are presented in LESA.

In the following, I will illustrate what is meant by this variety, providing a few examples from the lexicon, phonology, morphology, and syntax.

The LESA and *Fuṣḥā* forms are contrasted with those of the regional variety of Levantine known as rural Palestinian Arabic spoken in rural areas of northern Palestine. This will show, on the one hand, how regionalized features are suppressed in favor of the more standard urban LESA features and, on the other, how some *Fuṣḥā* features are abandoned in favor of this standard *'Āmmiyya* variety.[4]

Phonology

Different Levantine varieties have different sounds corresponding to the following *Fuṣḥā* consonants: th (ث), j, ð (ذ), ḍ (ض), ð̣ (ظ), q, k. Table 4.1 shows the *Fuṣḥā* consonants and their correspondences in a rural Palestinian variety and in LESA.[5]

Table 4.1

Fuṣḥā		*Rural Palestinian*	*LESA*
th	thalātha "three"	th	th, t
j	jāmiʿ "mosque"	j	j, ž
ð	ðahab "gold"	ð	ð, d, z
ḍ	ʿīd al-'aḍḥā "the feast of the Sacrifice"	ð̣	ḍ
ð̣	baʿd al-ð̣uhr "afternoon"	ð̣	ð̣, ḍ, ẓ
q	qāl "he said"	k	q, ʿ
k	kabīr "big"	ch	k

Morphology

Verbs based on "doubled" roots are conjugated differently in *Fuṣḥā* and the colloquial. LESA follows the colloquial pattern, as shown in Table 4.2.

Table 4.2

Fuṣḥā	*Rural Palestinian*	*LESA*	
huwa 'aḥassa	hū/huwwi ḥass	hū/huwwa ḥass	he felt
hiya 'aḥassat	hī/hiyyi ḥassat	hī/hiyya ḥassat	she felt
hum 'aḥassū	hummi ḥassū	humma/hummi ḥassū	they, m.p., felt
anta 'aḥsasta	inti ḥassēt	inta ḥassēt	you, m.s., felt
anti 'aḥsasti	inti ḥassēti	inti ḥassēti	you, f.s., felt
antum 'aḥsastum	intu ḥassētu	intu ḥassētu	you, m.p., felt
anā 'aḥsastu	ana ḥassēt	ana ḥassēt	I felt
naḥnu 'aḥsasnā	iḥna ḥassēna	iḥna/niḥna ḥassēna	we felt

Syntax (subject markers on the perfect verb)

Table 4.3

	Fuṣḥā	*Rural Palestinian*	*LESA*	
1	huwa sāfar	hū/huwwi sāfar	hū/huwwa sāfar	he traveled
2	hiya sāfarat	hī/hiyyi sāfarat	hī/hiyya sāfarat	she traveled
3	humā sāfarā	same as 5	same as 5	they, m.d., traveled
4	humā sāfaratā	same as 6	same as 5	they, f.d., traveled
5	hum sāfarū	hummi sāfarū	humma/hummi sāfarū	they, m.p., traveled
6	hunna sāfarna	hinni sāfarin	same as 5	they, f.p., traveled
7	anta sāfarta	inti sāfarit	inta sāfart	you, m.s., traveled
8	anti sāfarti	inti sāfarti	inti sāfarti	you, f.s., traveled
9	antumā sāfartumā	same as 10 and 11	same as 10	you, dual, common, traveled
10	antum sāfartum	intu sāfartu	intu sāfartu	you, m.p., traveled
11	antunna sāfartunna	intin sāfartin	same as 10	you, f.p., traveled
12	anā sāfartu	ana sāfarit	ana sāfart, sāfarit	I traveled
13	naḥnu sāfarnā	iḥna sāfarna	iḥna/niḥna sāfarna	we traveled

Lexicon

Table 4.4

Fuṣḥā	*Rural Palestinian*	*LESA*	
kāna	baka	kān	to be
'ayḍan	'ukhra	kamān	also
ḥakā	kharraf	ḥaka	to tell, relate a story
al-'ān	hassa	halla'	now
za'tar	dukka	za'tar	za'tar, thyme mixture
hāðā	hāða	hāða, hāda	this, m.
marra	nakli	marra	time, instance
ḥalaq	tarāchi	ḥalaq, ḥala'	earrings

Tables 4.1–4.4 confirm the views of a number of linguists cited in Chapter 1 about ESA, in this case LESA, where the grammatical base, particularly the morphology and syntax are fundamentally colloquial. Note for example, the conjugation of *huwa 'aḥassa/ḥass*, where rural Palestinian and LESA contrast with *Fuṣḥā*. Moreover, a look at the verb conjugation table (4.2) shows a clear deviation from the *Fuṣḥā* pattern, where maintaining the masculine/feminine distinction *hinni/hummi* and *intin/intu* of rural Palestinian would keep the forms closer to *Fuṣḥā*, since it also maintains that distinction, while the more prestigious LESA forms actually used do not. This shows, among other things, that the switch to the more prestigious does not always go in the direction of *Fuṣḥā*, but to the variety considered more prestigious for a certain linguistic phenomenon (See Ibrahim 1986; Abd-el-Jawad 1987).

Writing LESA

The principle of reflecting the sociolinguistic realities of Arabic is adhered to throughout the course of instruction and in the instructional materials. Since Arabs do not write *'Āmmiyya*, *'Āmmiyya* material is generally presented for listening and conversation and not for reading and writing practice. Writing, ranging from short answers to comprehension questions to long essays, takes place in *Fuṣḥā*.

A question that is often asked is, "How do you write *'Āmmiyya*, since there is no standard way of writing it?" The texts of the *'Āmmiyya* listening passages and video clips, found on the companion websites of the textbooks for the teachers to use as they present the material and for students to consult as a reference, are written in Arabic script. A phrase like قهوة أمريكيّة is written the same whether it is in a *Fuṣḥā* reading selection or in a *'Āmmiyya* conversation. It can be pronounced *qahwa 'amrīkiyya*, *qahwi 'amrīkiyyi*, or *'ahwi 'amrīkiyyi*, depending on the speaker and the context. Arabic speakers have no trouble providing the correct pronunciation in the appropriate context. There is some variation in the spelling of some *'Āmmiyya*-only words for which there is no standard spelling, such as مبارح/امبارح and أيوا/أيوه. But, again, native speakers have no trouble recognizing these words and pronouncing them correctly.

The alternative to using Arabic script is Roman transliteration, which, until recently, dominated the writing of *'Āmmiyya* books. I have addressed in detail the problems associated with using Roman transliteration in writing *'Āmmiyya* (Younes 1995c). Among the arguments put forth there are the following two: First, writing systems are optimally suited for the languages for which they are designed, and the Arabic writing system is no exception. Second, one important feature of all varieties of Arabic is what is called root-based morphology. Because the Arabic writing system is primarily consonant-based, roots can be identified and related to one another more easily if words are written in Arabic than in Roman transliteration because the latter typically includes all short vowels and treats all symbols on an equal footing, thus failing to capture the important role of the root. A third advantage to using Arabic script is mentioned by Al-Batal (1992: 299), who states, "The use of Arabic script helps students maintain the sense that they are dealing with one language, not two."

Related to the practical issue of writing LESA for pedagogical purposes is the wider issue of why it and other ESA varieties are not written. Ibrahim (1986: 121) compares what he calls Supra-Dialectal Low varieties (Levantine, Egyptian, Moroccan) to "such major varieties [of English] as standard British, American, and Australian English". The major difference in my opinion between the Arabic and English varieties lies in the fact that the Arabic varieties are only spoken; they are not permitted to be treated as both standard spoken and standard written. Any attempt at codifying the SDL varieties in the form of a comprehensive written grammar or in the form of textbooks is viewed as an infringement on the (sacred) territory of *Fuṣḥā*, the only legitimate written form. If the SDL varieties were codified and gained a foothold in the written world of Arabic, the *Fuṣḥā* monopoly on education, written communication, and most media would most likely come to an end, with the inevitable fate of being relegated to a religious language like Latin or Biblical Hebrew. Hence the stiff resistance to the codification and eventual recognition of the SDL varieties as fully standard in both the spoken and written spheres.

Another reason for the lack of codification of the SDL varieties may be that, as dynamic, living language forms in active use over large areas of the Arab world, there is a great deal of variability in comparison to *Fuṣḥā*, which has enjoyed remarkable stability for centuries due to religious, historical, and political reasons. This stability is demonstrated by the fact that Sībawyh's *al-Kitāb*, written in the eighth century, is still treated as a standard Arabic grammar reference.

Why integration makes sense[6]

The IA treats Arabic as one system of communication with two complementary sides, neither sufficient without the other for the range of communicative functions needed by the native Arabic speaker (Badawi 1985: 19–20), particularly if the educated native speaker is taken as the model for the learner in the AFL program, as is the case in foreign language instruction in general.

One may argue that other Arabic program structures, such as the introduction of the two varieties in two separate tracks, will produce the same results. While that may be possible, it involves unnecessary duplication and waste, creates an artificial division in the language, and deprives the learner of the opportunity to develop the skill to navigate the two language varieties as native speakers do.

On the basis of my experience building and teaching in an integrated program for over 23 years, I will now discuss these and other advantages of implementing an IA to Arabic language instruction. The typical objections raised against integration will be the topic of Chapter 5.

One course instead of two: building on shared features

It is a well-known fact that *ʿĀmmiyya* and *Fuṣḥā*, as varieties of the same language, share most of their vocabulary and grammatical structures (Ferguson 1959; Mansoor 1960: 90; Cadora 1976: 253). Since the language of education and most popular media (newspapers, radio and TV broadcasts, written literature, and scientific writing) is mostly *Fuṣḥā*, the higher the education level of an Arabic speaker, the richer the shared repertoire in terms of vocabulary and grammar. To give a numerical illustration of this phenomenon, I have counted the number of vocabulary items introduced in the three volumes of *ʿArabiyyat al-Naas*. Table 4.5 shows the number of *Fuṣḥā*-only, *ʿĀmmiyya*-only, and shared vocabulary items in the three volumes in terms of raw numbers and percentages.[7]

Two things are clear from this table. The first is that most of the vocabulary (between 81 percent and 92 percent) is shared between the two language varieties introduced in the textbook series. The second is that the ratio of shared vocabulary increases as the course progresses, reflecting the fact that

Table 4.5

	Number of new words	*Fuṣḥā only*	*ʿĀmmiyya only*	*Shared*
ʿArabiyyat al-Naas I	985	78 (7.9%)	106 (10.8%)	801 (81.5%)
ʿArabiyyat al-Naas II	1575	123 (7.8%)	52 (3.3%)	1400 (88.9%)
ʿArabiyyat al-Naas III	1419	86 (6%)	16 (1.1%)	1317 (92.8%)

variation seems to involve some of the most basic vocabulary of the two varieties, including high-frequency terms like *rāḥ/dhahaba, shāf/ra'ā, mish/laysa, kamān/'ayḍan*.

Once these terms are mastered, differences diminish drastically. This confirms the fact that *Fuṣḥā*, as the language of education, plays the role of a unifying force on the Arabic linguistic scene. We can also conclude that not only does education in *Fuṣḥā* bridge the gap between it and a colloquial variety, but it also bridges gaps between *ʿĀmmiyya* varieties, because of the increased amount of shared *Fuṣḥā* vocabulary.

In terms of the grammar, a look at the topics in the grammar index or in the table of contents of the three volumes shows that most of these topics are relevant in learning the two varieties. Is it not sufficient to introduce these grammatical features once and note the differences between the two varieties? Or should possession, verb conjugations, the *iḍāfa* construction and other grammatical phenomena be introduced once in the *ʿĀmmiyya* course and another time in the *Fuṣḥā* course? Consider, for example, possession in nouns, where a possessive pronoun is suffixed to a noun to indicate its possessor, one of the basic grammar features introduced in any introductory Arabic course. Table 4.6 shows the application of the rule in *Fuṣḥā* and *ʿĀmmiyya* (LESA).

Table 4.6

	Fuṣḥā	*ʿĀmmiyya*
His book	kitābu(hu)	kitābu(h)
Her book	kitābuha	kitābha
Their book	kitābuhum	kitābhum
Your, m.s., book	kitābuka	kitābak
Your, f.s., book	kitābuki	kitābik
Your, pl., book	kitābukum	kitābkum
My book	kitābi	kitābi
Our book	kitābuna	kitābna

In fact, the differences are even fewer than Table 4.6 shows. In an integrated program in which *Fuṣḥā* is introduced mainly for reading, particularly silent reading comprehension, and writing, differences involving short vowels disappear. This can best be illustrated by looking at the same table but with the Arabic words written in Arabic script (Table 4.7).

Table 4.7

	MSA	*Levantine*
His book	كتابه	كتابه
Her book	كتابها	كتابها
Their book	كتابهم	كتابهم
Your, m.s., book	كتابك	كتابك
Your, f.s., book	كتابك	كتابك
Your, pl., book	كتابكم	كتابكم
My book	كتابي	كتابي
Our book	كتابنا	كتابنا

As Table 4.7 shows, the forms have identical spelling. I am of course aware of the differences that the table does not show, such as the dual and feminine plural forms that are found in *Fuṣḥā* only, but these differences can be overlooked in an introductory Arabic course because of their relatively rare occurrence. When they arise later in a text, they can easily be explained with a short note. However, students do not need to learn them for active use in the first one or two semesters of their Arabic career.

Excursus: how people are more likely to notice differences than similarities

When we look at two cars side by side, one red and one blue, and are asked to describe them, the first thing that comes to mind is that one is red and the other blue. The two might be identical in every other respect, which means that they might share hundreds or thousands of components that are made from the same material by the same manufacturer, but such similarities are not the first thing that one notices.

The same is true of the phenomenon at hand, i.e. language varieties. When people compare Iraqi and Egyptian Arabic, for example, some of the first things that come to mind are differences, such as *shlōnak* in Iraqi compared to *izzayyak* in Egyptian for "How are you?" The fact that Egyptian and Iraqi Arabic share most of their consonant and vowel phonemes, the majority of their morphological patterns and syntactic structures, and the bulk of their vocabulary is not the first thing that comes to mind. If these two varieties did not share the overwhelming majority of these features, they would not be mutually intelligible.

Advocates of *Fuṣḥā* who have a negative view of *ʿĀmmiyya* tend to think more in terms of differences rather than shared features: They are quick to point out that *Fuṣḥā* has *laysa*, while *ʿĀmmiyya* has *mish*, overlooking the fact that the overwhelming majority of linguistic features are shared.

Madīni kbīri vs. madīnatun kabīratun, comprehension vs. production

The statistics in Table 4.5 above treat pairs of forms like those shown in Table 4.8 as the same in *Fuṣḥā* and *ʿĀmmiyya* (LESA).

Is one justified in such a treatment?

Table 4.8

F	*L*	
madīna(tun)	madīni	"city"
qāl	'āl	"he said"
ṣaghīr	zghīr	"small"
thalātha(tun)	talāti, thalāthi	"three"

The answer is "yes" for a number of reasons. For one thing, native speakers consider such pairs of forms identical, and our goal should be to develop in the learner the native speaker's competence in the language. As Williams (1990: 46) put it, "if variation is inherent in language, it is perhaps less disconcerting for the student if he is introduced to variation earlier rather than later".

It might be instructive here to draw a distinction between linguistic investigation and pedagogical considerations. While the student of linguistics is drawn to and is mainly interested in differences and variation, the reader/listener is interested in the message being communicated and will use the information available to decipher that message. For example, in an exchange between a fruit seller and a buyer, both sides would be much more interested in whether to pay or receive three dinars than in the fact that either side said *thalāthi*, *talāti*, *thalātha*, *talāta*, or *tlēti*. The context and the information provided, even if there is a difference between the way the interlocutors pronounce the word, determine the success of communication. So while the linguist would listen to the differences between *thalātha* and *talāti*, the practical communicator would be interested in whether the message is successfully conveyed and would use the shared sounds of the variant forms and the context to achieve successful communication.

Given sufficient linguistic and extra-linguistic information, students can learn patterns of difference and are able to comprehend a message that is delivered in a manner different from the one in which they would deliver it or they had heard or read before. One piece of evidence to support this claim is that students with an advanced mastery of one variety of Arabic, such as Egyptian, are able to function successfully in another, such as Levantine.

Many phonological, morphological, and syntactic differences between the two language varieties can be learned through simple rules and with sufficient examples. The student can learn through such examples that *'* and *t* of LESA often correspond to *q* and *th* of *Fuṣḥā*.

To sum up, linguistic differences between *'Āmmiyya* and *Fuṣḥā* are far outweighed by the similarities, and since most differences are predictable from one variety to the other, it makes sense to introduce the two to the foreign learner once in one track rather than twice in two separate tracks.

No need to divide the indivisible

Having two separate tracks, one for *Fuṣḥā* and another for *'Āmmiyya*, regardless of when each variety is introduced, requires a decision about which material to introduce in each track. As has been pointed out, the majority of linguistic material is shared by the two language varieties.[8] Judging by the vocabulary and grammar introduced in the *'Arabiyyat al-Naas* series, the difference between LESA and *Fuṣḥā* in terms of the vocabulary ranges between 10 percent and 20 percent. The decision to assign two separate tracks would be made on the basis of the smaller difference rather than on the much larger set of shared elements.

While it is easy to assign *mish*, *shāf*, and *kamān* to the *'Āmmiyya* track, and their *Fuṣḥā* equivalents *laysa*, *ra'ā*, and *'ayḍan* to the *Fuṣḥā* track, it is impossible to assign most (80–90 percent) of the vocabulary to one or the other without a certain amount of duplication and waste. The same applies to grammar. While it is relatively easy to assign the case and mood systems only to the *Fuṣḥā* track, the systems of possession, verb conjugation, verbs forms, and the construct are not easily distinguished.

Preparing the learner to deal effectively with the relationship between the two language varieties

As Ferguson put it in 1959 and as is still valid today, "it is typical behavior to have someone read aloud from a newspaper written in H (*Fuṣḥā*) and then proceed to discuss the contents in L (*'Āmmiyya*)". And as Badawi wrote in 1973 (Badawi 1973: 150), a university professor reads his lecture notes in *Fuṣḥā* but discusses the contents of his lecture in *'Āmmiyya*.

Arabic speakers, particularly educated speakers, have access to the two varieties and use each in its proper context spontaneously and for the most part effortlessly. The examples of the newspaper and the university lecture are only two in a general pattern of linguistic behavior. The two varieties of the language are in constant contact and use: watching and discussing the news, reading and discussing an article in a classroom, reading the menu in a restaurant and ordering food from it, or discussing the topic of a religious sermon with a friend or a family member.

When *Fuṣḥā* and *'Āmmiyya* are introduced separately, the learner is deprived of the opportunity to develop the crucial sociolinguistic skill of using each variety in its proper context. One can read about this skill and discuss it in theory, but to master it for use in real life the learner needs practice with real language: the Arabic classroom and the Arabic instructional materials can provide the first real training.

Reinforcement

The IA makes possible the creation of a natural, communicative classroom environment in which actual linguistic behavior can be reflected in the classroom in the form of actual and realistic conversations between teacher and students and among the students themselves. Unlike an approach that introduces *Fuṣḥā* and uses it for all language skills, the typical pattern in AFL programs, the IA frees the Arabic teacher from the forced and burdensome obligation of using

Fuṣḥā for conversation. Arabs themselves have trouble conversing in *Fuṣḥā* about basic, everyday matters, not necessarily because they do not master the skill, but because they do not use this variety of the language for such functions in real life. Conversing in *ʿĀmmiyya* is more comfortable for teachers and helps create an environment that is more conducive to real and meaningful verbal communication between teacher and students. Based on my own observations, for most teachers, using *Fuṣḥā* for conversation is a tense experience that typically makes it hard to focus on the message, since attention is focused on the form of the language, particularly the correct use of case and mood endings. This is probably why there is the widespread feeling that teachers do not speak enough Arabic in the classroom (Lampe 1985: 11; Haddad 1985: 17).

In discussing the different possible scenarios for teaching diglossic languages, Ferguson (1971: 73) raises the issue of language maintenance. He asks, "[H]ow can skill in one variety be maintained when the learning is concentrated on the other variety?" In the integrated program, maintenance is not a problem since neither side of the language is developed at the expense of the other or in its absence; rather, the two are developed equally and simultaneously.

Richer, more varied, and more interesting classroom environment

The IA makes possible the unrestricted use of high-quality, pedagogically effective, and interesting instructional materials from both varieties of the language, including poems, short stories, and articles written in *Fuṣḥā*, as well as songs, folktales, and plays that use *ʿĀmmiyya* as their medium. Introducing both types of material into the classroom enriches the students' experience and provides needed variety that breaks the near monopoly of newspaper articles and news broadcasts in *Fuṣḥā*-only classes,[9] on the one hand, and conversations at the airport, at the restaurant, and at the pharmacy, a common feature of *ʿĀmmiyya*-only textbooks and *ʿĀmmiyya*-only classes, on the other.

Simpler grammar[10]

Finally, in a truly integrated program, students learn to use certain aspects of Arabic grammar actively for conversation, while they learn other aspects found only in *Fuṣḥā* for passive recognition or for use in writing. As examples, let us consider negation and verb conjugation, two basic features of Arabic grammar in any Arabic course. In a course where *Fuṣḥā* is introduced for all skills, including speaking, students are taught to negate equational (verbless) sentences with *laysa*, which is fully conjugated in 13 persons, as shown in Table 4.9.

In an integrated course in which *ʿĀmmiyya* is used for conversation and *Fuṣḥā* for reading, writing, and formal speech, the student would learn to use the one form *mish* (which in some varieties is pronounced *mush* and in others replaced by *mū*) for conversation and would learn to recognize the various forms of *laysa* for other uses.

Table 4.9

1	laysa	He is not
2	laysat	She is not
3	laysā	They, m.d., are not
4	laysatā	They, f.d., are not
5	laysū	They, m.p., are not
6	lasna	They, f.p., are not
7	lasta	You, m.s., are not
8	lasti	You, f.s., are not
9	lastumā	You, common d., are not
10	lastum	You, m.p., are not
11	lastunna	You, f.p., are not
12	lastu	I am not
13	lasnā	We are not

The same can be said of verb conjugations in general. Most major *'Āmmiyya* varieties (e.g. LESA, Egyptian) have eight forms while *Fuṣḥā* has 13. Why should the foreign student learn to use the dual and feminine plural for conversation, when the native speaker himself or herself does not?

Notes

1 In addition to failing to take advantage of the benefits of an integrated approach listed below in the section "Why integration makes sense" (building on shared features, no need to divide the indivisible, preparing the learner to deal effectively with the relationship between the two language varieties, and a richer and varied classroom environment), a major problem with beginning with *'Āmmiyya* exclusively is that, in order for the program and the instructional materials to be a true reflection of the realities of the Arabic sociolinguistic situation, the focus of the Arabic course would be on listening and speaking while the reading and writing skills would have to wait until *Fuṣḥā* is introduced. This overlooks the fact that, unlike Arab pre-school children, students in Arabic-as-a-foreign-language programs can, as educated adult learners, use their ability to read and write to reinforce the other skills. And since we are dealing with the same language with the majority of linguistic features shared by the two varieties, reading and writing can play a key role in helping master new material.

2 I would like to point out that the IA is designed for AFL learners who are interested in mastering the four language skills (listening, speaking, reading, and writing) relevant for mastery of Arabic as used by Arabic speakers in the modern Arab world and not for learners with specialized interests such as understanding the language of the Qur'ān.

3 This phenomenon is referred to by Blanc (1960) as "leveling" and "classicizing" devices. See also Mitchell (1990: 19).

4 For more features characteristic of LESA, see Haddad 1985: 18–21 and Ryding 1991: 215.

5 On the suppression of certain phonological features of rural Palestinian and Jordanian dialects in favor of a standard urban variety, see Abd-el-Jawad (1986). The rich phonology of LESA confirms Elverskog's statement about Badawi's *'Āmmiyyat al-muthaqqafīn* (ESA) as "the richest language level in terms of the number of sounds it engages" (Elverskog 1999: 42).

6 Al-Batal (1992: 301) lists the following four advantages for the Integrated Approach: "it will (1) offer language that is truly authentic in both contexts and function and make our Arabic programs proficiency-oriented in the fullest sense; (2) place more emphasis on the communicative skills in Arabic and make the learning of structure more context-based, which will render the process of learning Arabic a more lively and meaningful experience, not merely an intellectual pursuit; (3) provide a well-rounded language program that fulfills most needs of our students, most of whom, since they want to communicate with Arabs using a natural medium, as well as read texts, would like to see more speaking done in the classroom ... ; (4) enhance, through its inclusion of the colloquial, the cultural component of our Arabic curriculum."

7 In the comprehensive glossaries of the three volumes of the series, *Fuṣḥā*-only words such as *'ayḍan*, *al-'ān*, *dhahaba*, etc. and colloquial-only words such as *kamān*, *halla'*, and *raaḥ* are marked by different symbols, while shared words are not marked.

8 Bassiouney (2009: 55) writes "ECA (Egyptian Colloquial Arabic) and MSA (*Fuṣḥā*) are different codes but with a lot of shared content and system morphemes and it is almost impossible to say whether a certain morpheme belongs to ECA or to MSA." (See also p. 163.)

9 The following comment by Abboud (1971: 7) still applies to much of the *Fuṣḥā* materials currently used in Arabic textbooks: "The subject matter and cultural content of many MSA books leave much to be desired. Basic texts for the most part are grammar oriented; liveliness and naturalness are here sacrificed to simplicity of structure. With few exceptions, most materials deal with political topics, which for the most part are monotonous, very quickly outdated, and unchallenging to all but a few." This is simply the nature of *Fuṣḥā*, which does not really reflect Arab life and culture the way *'Āmmiyya* does.

10 Ferguson (1959: 334) states that the following generalization applies to at least three of the four defining languages in his study, namely Arabic, Greek, and Haitian Creole: "the grammatical structure of any given L (here *'Āmmiyya*) variety is simpler than that of its corresponding H (here *Fuṣḥā*). See also Kaye (1972: 40–1) where he gives examples to demonstrate that "Cairo Arabic (or any C[olloquial] for that matter) has 'simplified' the system [of MSA] considerably", and Zughoul (1980: 205), who states that "Colloquial Arabic is simpler than FA (*Fuṣḥā*) in syntax and lexicon."

5 Objections to Integration

Two main objections have been raised against integrating *Fuṣḥā* and *'Āmmiyya* in the same course of instruction. The first revolves around the issue of which of the many *'Āmmiyya* varieties is to be chosen in an integrated program, and the second is fear of confusing learners. I will address these two issues in this chapter.

Which dialect?[1]

The issue of whether or not to teach *'Āmmiyya*, and which *'Āmmiyya* variety to teach, has been widely debated (Parkinson 1985: 27; Shiri 2013: 565 and references there). The choice of *'Āmmiyya* itself is not as much a challenge to integration as a challenge to the introduction of *'Āmmiyya* in the Arabic program in any form. Nevertheless, since one of the main features of the IA is the introduction of *'Āmmiyya*, I will address this issue in some detail, using my experience in an integrated program as a guide.

The *'Āmmiyya* question is generally couched in one of two ways: first, there are so many *'Āmmiyya* varieties; not only does every country have its own *'Āmmiyya*, but variation exists between one city or one village and another and even one neighborhood and another in the same city. Which variety should one choose in an Arabic program? Second, since we don't know which Arab country our students will end up visiting, if they go at all, how can we decide on one *'Āmmiyya* variety and not another?

This issue has political, financial, and practical implications. If Egyptian Arabic is chosen in an Arabic program, then Egypt is given more recognition than other Arab countries, and Egyptian teachers will have a better chance of getting a job than their Tunisian counterparts, for example. In other cases, instructional resources are much more readily available in some *'Āmmiyya* varieties than others, or certain programs have teachers with different *'Āmmiyya* backgrounds. How can we introduce Levantine in a program that has teachers from Egypt, Libya, and Sudan?

The standard "solution" is to introduce *Fuṣḥā* and use it as a foundation for learning a dialect later. Learning a dialect will be easy then, so the argument runs. For example, Al-Hamad (1983: 95) states:

> My students who showed a desire to study a dialect found wonderful psychological relief when I gave them the analogy of the high language [being] like the peak of a mountain and the dialects like its numerous low sides, and [when] I showed them that we seek to take them to the peak because after that they could descend to the lower [sides] if they so desired. Our interest in one dialect over another makes reaching the peak difficult.

According to Abed and Sawan (2011: xix), "[W]ith a firm grounding in *Faṣīḥ* [the name they give to modern, simplified *Fuṣḥā*], students can branch out to learn the local dialects of countries where they visit or reside."

Again a distinction between linguistic investigation and pedagogical need is fundamental. It makes sense for a linguist who specializes in Arabic dialectology to be interested in the smallest differences among the various *ʿĀmmiyya*s. The pedagogue, on the other hand, whose goal is to help prepare the language learner to function successfully in as much of the Arabic-speaking world as possible, is looking for major dialect groups or "standard" *ʿĀmmiyya*s. Identifying a standard *ʿĀmmiyya* variety is one step toward simplifying the search for the right *ʿĀmmiyya* variety. Rather than being confronted with a choice of three or four (or even more) Egyptian *ʿĀmmiyya*s, we can focus on the one variety that is considered standard for Egypt. And rather than having to choose between urban Palestinian, rural Palestinian, urban Jordanian, Bedouin Jordanian, Aleppo Syrian, Damascene Syrian, etc. we can focus on a major Levantine variety of *ʿĀmmiyya*.

For AFL programs in Arabic-speaking countries the choice of *ʿĀmmiyya* should be straightforward: students should be introduced to the standard *ʿĀmmiyya* variety of the country or region they are in – generally the *ʿĀmmiyya* of the capital city.

For programs outside the Arab world, the *ʿĀmmiyya* choice is naturally more complicated. For Cornell's integrated Arabic program, I have chosen what I called in the previous chapter Levantine Educated Spoken Arabic (LESA). It is the variety used by educated speakers of the Levantine area (Jordan, Palestine, Syria, and Lebanon) when communicating with one another and with speakers of other varieties of Arabic. It is the Levantine version of what has been termed, among other things, Educated Spoken Arabic, Supra-dialectal Low (SDL), *ʿĀmmiyyat al-muthaqqafīn, al-lugha al-wusṭā* (see Ryding 1991: 213).[2]

Previous attempts at introducing ESA in the Arabic classroom

This, of course, is not the first attempt to introduce this "intermediate" variety into the Arabic classroom. Haddad (1985: 17) wrote a textbook called *al-'Arabiyya al-Maḥkiyya* (*Spoken Arabic*), which was meant to be "an effective means to aid students to use what they learned in *Fuṣḥā* in a manner acceptable to and understandable by the educated Arab of the eastern part of the Arab world (*al-Mashriq*)". She adds that

> the student who has studied *Fuṣḥā* for two or more years is able to express himself and transition from *Fuṣḥā* to spoken Arabic. But before this transition process the student needs to take a course in Spoken Arabic which allows him to be acquainted with its features and to practice using its phrases, expressions and styles in a practical and acceptable manner … .
>
> (Ibid.)

The spoken Arabic included in the textbook, according to Haddad, is what can be called "the third, common, middle language, a phenomenon found among educated people in Arab countries whose existence has grown and spread" (ibid.: 16–17).

As was mentioned in Chapter 4, Nicola (1990: 42) advocates starting "with Educated Spoken Arabic (ESA), then proceed[ing] with the written language while using ESA for speaking all the time".

Ryding (1991: 212, 217) describes a program at the Foreign Service Institute (FSI) where Formal Spoken Arabic (FSA) "is normally taught concurrently with MSA, so that students develop their ability to converse along with their ability to read … " and where "a normal day might consist of three to four classroom hours of FSA in the morning and two hours of MSA in the afternoon". According to Ryding, FSA

> is not the vernacular of a circumscribed geographical region, but nonetheless represents a real segment of the continuum of spoken Arabic variants – a supra-regional, prestige form of spoken Arabic practical as a means of communication throughout the Arabic-speaking world. It is also referred to as Educated Spoken Arabic (ESA) in much of the research literature. In this paper I shall use "FSA" as a term which includes ESA.

Badawi on the teaching of ESA and MSA

Badawi (1985: 20) argues against teaching ESA varieties to the foreign learner because it is "inherently difficult to work out a complete system" of them due to their lack of stability, and he recommends the teaching of MSA, which is its written version (ibid.: 21). In an attempt to minimize the difference between ESA and MSA, Badawi (ibid.) states that

> the distance between ESA and MSA, once the latter is examined on its own merits and not in the light of the work of the old Arab grammarians, will be discovered to be not as great as is currently supposed. For instance, we will come to recognize the observable fact that the cumbersome system of vowel endings, to which we still insist on subjecting learners of MSA, is actually redundant.

As has been made clear in this and other chapters of the book, one of the main objections to introducing *Fuṣḥā* (*Fuṣḥā al-'aṣr* or MSA in Badawi's case) only or primarily to the foreign learner is the insistence on using it for all language skills, including conversation. While the "cumbersome system of vowel endings" of *Fuṣḥā* is of minor importance to the student who is reading Arabic, it is nevertheless essential in using the language correctly from a grammatical point of view. Conversing in *Fuṣḥā* and using incorrect *i'rāb* (system of case and mood assignment) is grammatically unacceptable. In MSA, simple questions like "What's your name" or "How many children do you have?" must respect the rules of case: "*Mā ismak*?" and "*Kam walad 'indak*?" are incorrect. This is why trying to get around the problem by renaming *Fuṣḥā* as *Faṣīḥ* (Abed and Sawan 2011: Introduction) and using it for conversation faces the same problem. *Faṣīḥ* is a version of *Fuṣḥā* with its *i'rāb* system and other aspects of grammar not used for conversation.

Badawi's objections to the teaching of ESA, due to its instability, are not without validity. In contrast with MSA, which has abundant grammars and texts of all types, ESA has not been codified and its rules have not been systematically described. In the absence of a detailed description, a written grammar and a set of textbooks that set them apart from *Fuṣḥā* and non-standard *'Āmmiyya* varieties, ESA varieties, including LESA, may be viewed as "the interplay between *Fuṣḥā* and *'Āmmiyya* (Mitchell 1986: 7), with a high ratio of *Fuṣḥā* vocabulary and a fundamentally *'Āmmiyya* base in morphology and syntax, as was shown in chapters 1 and 4.

Why LESA?

LESA was chosen for the integrated program at Cornell University for four main reasons:

1 It is a major *'Āmmiyya* variety that is actively used by speakers from the Levantine area, and, as is the case with other major colloquial varieties, such as Egyptian, is understood over a large area outside of it. In Ibrahim's words (1986: 121) "Like SDH (Supra-Dialectal High = *Fuṣḥā*), varieties of SDL (Supra-Dialectal Low, e.g. LESA, Egyptian) are mutually intelligible. It is also probably true that SDL is understood by a majority of Arabic speakers in countries where no SDL varieties are spoken" (see also Badawi 1985: 15). In addition, this variety of the language is spreading as evidenced by the fact that "the younger generation [is] showing a much wider use of SDL features than their parents" (Ibrahim 1986: 121).
2 Together with Egyptian, LESA seems to be the most popular choice for American and, probably, most foreign students of Arabic who have shown an interest in learning *'Āmmiyya*. According to Al-Batal and Belnap "[R]ecent NMELRC (National Middle East Language Resource Center) surveys indicate that 86 percent of students who expressed interest in learning Spoken Arabic prefer either Levantine or Egyptian Arabic" (Al-Batal and Belnap 2006: 396). A survey by Shiri (2013: 576) confirms this statement: "Most of those [students] who suggest particular

dialects specifically singled out Levantine (12 percent) or Egyptian (12 percent), or both (30 percent) as the widely understood or widely useful dialects."

3 If we consider the fact that speakers of the Maghribi (Moroccan, Algerian, Tunisian) varieties tend to accommodate speakers of the Arab East (Egyptian and Levantine) in cross-dialectal verbal interaction, as documented in another study by Shiri (2002), then students who have mastered Levantine (or Egyptian) will likely be able to communicate with speakers of Maghribi dialects as well.

4 While Egyptian Arabic may have more speakers than LESA and may be understood over a larger area of the Arab world, I have chosen Levantine for the practical reason that it is the *ʿĀmmiyya* variety that I, as a teacher and curriculum developer, am most familiar with, that I have studied extensively, and that I am comfortable using.

Dialect-neutrality

One of the arguments put forth in favor of teaching *Fuṣḥā* as opposed to *ʿĀmmiyya* is the desire to be "dialect-neutral" (Ryding 1991: 213). The implication is that association with a dialect region is to be avoided. There is of course no doubt that conversing in LESA would suggest that the foreign student has learned Arabic in a program in which Levantine is used for conversation. But why should that be treated differently from a foreign learner of American English who uses that variety for conversation in the United Kingdom?

In fact, it does not really matter which major *ʿĀmmiyya* variety is introduced. A high level of proficiency in one is sufficient for communication with speakers, especially educated speakers, of other major varieties, as evidenced by students who master Egyptian Arabic and visit or live in the Levant or Iraq, and students who master Levantine and visit or live in Egypt. (See student testimonials below.) On the other hand, students who have studied any Arabic variety, be it *Fuṣḥā* or *ʿĀmmiyya*, for one or two semesters cannot be expected to communicate easily with speakers of any variety.

Students who have learned to converse in LESA in Cornell's integrated program and who have reached a high level of proficiency in the language were comfortable using it in the Levantine area as well as in other areas of the Arab world.

Students who traveled to Egypt reported that they faced some problems initially but after figuring out some of the basic phonological differences were able to communicate successfully. Here are some student testimonials.

Student testimonials[3]

Following are testimonials by five graduates of Cornell's integrated Arabic program who had the opportunity to deal with speakers of Arabic varieties other than LESA:

1

Overall, I feel as though my experience learning in Cornell's Arabic program, as opposed to alternative programs that focus solely on MSA, was greatly beneficial and helped me to adapt to new linguistic challenges. When I first lived abroad in Jordan, it was a matter of getting used to the speech of native speakers. Later, when I moved to Egypt, the challenge was to re-align my linguistic expectations to suit the Egyptian dialect and its particular vocabulary, pronunciation, stress patterns, syntax, etc. In both cases, I felt as though my background in a dialect provided me with a mental representation of Arabic that I could continuously shape and re-shape as I learned more about the language. Having studied a spoken form of Arabic also made me more aware and a better "noticer" of certain meta-linguistic elements, such as hand gestures and body language, as well as the linguistic strategies that native speakers use to carry out different speech acts, such as thanking, giving advice, or changing topics.

(Priscilla Cunha, Cornell University, 2010. Currently MA student, Department of Middle Eastern Studies, University of Texas, Austin)

2

After studying Levantine Arabic for two years in Cornell's Arabic Program, I spent a summer in Egypt. Although several teachers at Cornell had exposed me to a variety of dialects (Palestinian, Iraqi, Jordanian, etc.) in addition to the Levantine variety we studied in class, I had had little – if any – exposure to Egyptian prior to that summer. Many of the other passengers on my plane to Cairo were also Arabic students; we were all so excited to use our language in the "real world" that we immediately started chatting up the airport employees and random folks in the airport.

For the first time in my life, I heard the MSA phrase "*mā ismuka*?" being spoken aloud. The well-meaning students around me were all being met with looks of confusion and even laughter from the Egyptian people they tried to engage in MSA. My own Levantine "*shu ismak*" was met with the expected reply "ismī … [name]"; after we exchanged a few more pleasantries, I was asked whether I was from Lebanon or Jordan … .

For my Egyptian Colloquial Arabic (ECA) section, I was in a small class with only one other student and the teacher. In the first few weeks, I struggled a little bit with differences in basic vocabulary, phonology, and morphology. In general, though, no one seemed to have a problem understanding my strong Levantine lilt; nor did I ever hit a complete communicative barrier when someone spoke to me in Egyptian.

After those two months, my Arabic was in a sort of transitional phase between Levantine and Egyptian, and my third year of Arabic at Cornell pulled this in the direction of MSA, with courses in media, literature, and Qur'anic Arabic. However, my dialect became thoroughly Egyptian when I moved to Egypt after graduating.

Now in grad school at UT Austin, I interact on a daily basis with colleagues and professors with diverse Arabic backgrounds: Syria, Jordan, Palestine, Egypt, Lebanon, Iraq, etc. There are seemingly no communicative barriers.

(Ryan Fan, Cornell, 2010. Currently PhD candidate, Department of Middle Eastern Languages and Cultures, University of Texas, Austin.)

3

Cornell's integrated Arabic program prepared me well to communicate with speakers of other dialects. The emphasis placed on conversation practice meant that we grew comfortable speaking in colloquial Arabic, learning distinctions between *Fuṣḥā* and colloquial Levantine Arabic early on. After studying the Levantine dialect at Cornell I spent time in Egypt, and found it easy to communicate with Egyptians. I was almost always understood while speaking Levantine to Egyptians, and could use Levantine to understand many aspects of the Egyptian dialect. While Egyptians were sometimes surprised to hear a foreigner speaking Levantine, they could certainly understand it.

(Jacob Arem, Cornell 2011. Currently Research Assistant at a think tank in Washington, DC)

4

Learning Arabic through Cornell's integrated approach allowed me to transition to learning the Iraqi Arabic dialect, and has facilitated my communication with speakers of other Arabic dialects. After graduating from Cornell's program, I had both *Fuṣḥā* and Levantine Arabic to draw on, which I could use as a reference point in speaking with people who spoke different Arabic dialects. By having knowledge of both *Fuṣḥā* and Levantine, it gave me a greater pool of vocabulary to draw on and a way to understand the similarities that exist across dialects. Native speakers of other dialects never had any difficulty understanding me, and I understood them because of my wide vocabulary pool, and my exposure, through Cornell's diverse staff, to various Arabic dialects. Additionally, having dialectal experience allowed me to communicate with Arabic native speakers who were not trained in *Fuṣḥā* and were more comfortable speaking in their own native dialect.

(Ian Gillen, Cornell 2011. Currently MA student in Middle Eastern Studies, University of Texas, Austin)

5

Since I began learning Arabic, I've done a fair amount of traveling throughout the Arab world and also in Europe. In my travels I have encountered speakers of all different dialects – Jordanian, Palestinian, Syrian, Lebanese, Egyptian, Sudanese, Algerian, Tunisian, Moroccan, and Gulf Arabic – and I do not remember a single instance when I was unable to communicate with someone. My accent seems to be understood easily by educated native speakers, regardless of their origin, and as soon as they hear me speak *shami* dialect they tend to adjust their word choice to help me understand. Occasionally, I have to ask speakers of North African dialects to repeat or rephrase themselves, but I have no problem understanding Gulf Arabic or anything from *bilad al-sham.*

(Emily Koppelman, Cornell 2013. Currently Communications and Student Affairs Manager at Al-Mashriq Center for Arabic Instruction, Amman, Jordan)

How many dialects should a student learn?

When asked the question "How many dialects should a student learn?", the first response that comes to my mind is "How many dialects of English should one learn to function in that language?"

For the practical needs of the foreign learner, there is no need to learn more than one major *'Āmmiyya* variety. As I have tried to show above, mastering one such variety should equip the student to function in the Arabic-speaking world in the same way that a student of American English would function in the United Kingdom or Australia. (See also Abboud 1971: 5, who states that "with firm control of one dialect, the student should be able, after a period of adjustment, to communicate with speakers of another".)

If *'Āmmiyya* is approached in the manner advocated in this book, i.e. as a major variety, considered the spoken standard in the same way that standard American or Standard British English is (Ibrahim 1986: 121), then Arabic ceases to be an exotic and difficult language with many different dialects, each of which needs to be learned separately. Consider the following inadvertently patronizing statement made by an Arabic student in a study-abroad program about Arabic "slang", quoted by Shiri (2013: 576): "I think it's important to learn as many dialects as possible ... people from the Arab world are always pleased when you know their local slang. I met Egyptians in Jordan that were so happy I knew some Egyptian colloquial Arabic."

Can a teacher teach a dialect that is not his or her own?

Another challenge to Arabic programs that introduce *'Āmmiyya* is the practical issue of whether a teacher whose native *'Āmmiyya* is Iraqi, for example, is able to teach Egyptian or Levantine. Naturally one cannot assume that a speaker of one variety is both able and willing to speak in a manner different from his or her own. However, there are a number of related issues that should be taken into account.

First, one should think of the alternatives. Is the option of conversing in *Fuṣḥā*, which is not used for conversation, a better alternative? Which would be more comfortable for a teacher to use for conversation, *Fuṣḥā* or a dialect other than his or her own? The answers to such questions may vary from one teacher to another.

The answer to this question is related to what is meant by *'Āmmiyya*. Asking an Iraqi teacher to teach the *'Āmmiyya* variety referred to in the previous section as LESA is more realistic than asking him or her to teach the variety described as rural Palestinian Arabic. For one thing it is closer to the Arabic variety this teacher already knows, and for another, teaching the localized form of a dialect with its socially stigmatized features will sound strange and pretentious.

Since the integrated program was started at Cornell in 1990, teachers with Jordanian, Lebanese, Palestinian, Syrian, Iraqi, Kuwaiti, Egyptian, Sudanese, Tunisian, Moroccan, and American English backgrounds have taught in it. The teachers who spoke a variety other than LESA have not found it difficult to teach in the program, for two main reasons. First, the existence of a textbook that can be described as teacher- and student-friendly has helped define their role and provide the "script" for that role. Second, the focus on LESA, which suppresses regionalisms and maximizes shared standard forms, including words, expressions, and sounds, shrinks the gap between these varieties and eliminates many of the differences among them.

Of course teachers sometimes felt more comfortable using a high-frequency form found in their own *'Āmmiyya* variety but not in LESA. For example, when an Iraqi teacher felt uncomfortable using *biddi* "I want", he was encouraged to use *'arīd*, with which he was more comfortable, and to explain to the students that that is the form used by Iraqi speakers. While some might think that introducing both *biddi* and *'arīd* is confusing, I would note that when asked about this phenomenon students generally thought that it was to their advantage to hear some of the most common *'Āmmiyya* variants. It should, however, be re-emphasized that words like *'arīd* and *biddi* are a minority compared to the majority of shared words.

One possibility that might work well in some programs, particularly programs that offer several levels of Arabic, is to assign teachers who are not native speakers of the *'Āmmiyya* variety introduced in the program to teach higher level courses. As was shown above, the gap between *Fuṣḥā* and *'Āmmiyya* shrinks as more material characteristic of the language of education is introduced. A comparison of the listening materials and written texts and activities of *'Arabiyyat al-Nās* III with those of *'Arabiyyat al-Nās* I illustrates this point clearly.

Finally, cautioning the reader that "the issue remains a sensitive one ideologically" (Abdalla and Al-Batal 2011–12: 17) report that "most teachers (60 percent) are willing to teach and feel comfortable teaching the basics of a dialect that is not their native one".

Confusion

Arguing against the incorporation of *'Āmmiyya* into a *Fuṣḥā* class, Parkinson wrote:

> It is very difficult to incorporate Colloquial into a Standard Arabic class without leaving the students hopelessly confused. Arabic is hard enough

> without having to remember almost from the first day that you can say *mish* but you can't write it.[4]
>
> (Parkinson 1985: 27; see also Rammuny 1993: 11)

The power of the "confusion argument" lies in its intuitive appeal: how can students be introduced to two (or more) forms of the same word or expression and be expected to use each in its proper context? (Shiri 2013: 567). Naturally things should be made simple and clear to students. No teacher would want to confuse his/her students with different forms of the same word or two systems of negation. However, if we subject the confusion argument to deeper scrutiny, much of its power vanishes, particularly if set against the practices in the profession as a whole. The most common such practice followed in the overwhelming majority of Arabic programs is the use of *Fuṣḥā* for all language skills, including conversation. Students are thus taught to say the wrong forms throughout the course. Although the word "confusion", when used in connection with an integrated approach, might carry heavy negative connotations and might be in some cases an unavoidable consequence of the attempt to prepare students to deal effectively with Arabic sociolinguistic realities, the practice of teaching *Fuṣḥā* for conversation should be viewed as consciously and deliberately misleading students by teaching them to use the wrong forms in certain situations.

Another common practice that may be more confusing to Arabic students than integration is the introduction of an activity in *Fuṣḥā* along with its translation in *'Āmmiyya*. For example, in the "story" part of Lesson 2 of the first volume of *Al-Kitaab fii Ta'allum al-'Arabiyya* (2004), the most widely used Arabic-as-a-foreign-language textbook today, students are taught to identify themselves and to talk about family and work in *Fuṣḥā*. In the *'Āmmiyya* part of the same lesson, they are taught to do the exact same thing in Egyptian Arabic. If I were an Arabic student, I would ask why should I learn both? If I can introduce myself in Egyptian Arabic, when am I supposed to use the other version? For the the Arabic speaker, *'Āmmiyya* and the colloquial *complement*, not *duplicate*, each other.

Potential confusion of some *Fuṣḥā* and *'Āmmiyya* forms by students of Arabic may be viewed as a less serious problem if considered in the wider context of a well-designed Arabic curriculum. The use of appropriate forms in the right context is a skill that develops along with mastery of the language, whatever the language may be. Errors, whether linguistic or sociolinguistic, are expected at all levels of language learning, regardless of the approach followed. No approach guarantees error-free performance by learners, linguistically or sociolinguistically. Making mistakes is an integral part of the learning process.[5]

Confusion of *Fuṣḥā* and *'Āmmiyya* is minimized in the integrated program because of the way the two varieties are presented in integrated textbooks and introduced in the classroom: *Fuṣḥā* materials are presented in the form of passages to be read and understood but not to be actively spoken. *'Āmmiyya* materials are introduced and regularly used as a foundation for speaking activities. Experience shows that students develop a sense for the appropriate use of *Fuṣḥā* and the colloquial at a surprisingly early stage in their learning of the language. For example, I have personally observed that by the end of the first semester, or after 70 hours of classroom instruction, my students are able to tell that the *'Āmmiyya* word *ḥāmi* "hot" is used in speaking while its *Fuṣḥā* counterpart *ḥārr* is used in writing, and they write *ḥārr* in their compositions and use *ḥāmī* when conversing about the weather. Distinctions between forms acceptable only in writing and others acceptable only in speaking are common to all languages. The concept and the practice are familiar and not unique to Arabic.

The "confusion" argument might well be the result of an exaggerated concern on the part of teachers to protect their students from being overwhelmed, while students might in fact be more capable than their teachers give them credit for. If this is the case, then teachers would be doing their students a disservice by not preparing them for the sociolinguistic realities of Arabic while thinking they are helping them.

Notes

1 For a discussion of factors that may play a role in the choice of which *'Āmmiyya* variety to teach, see Abboud (1971: 5).

2 Ryding (1991: 214) criticizes the use of the term Educated Spoken Arabic because, in her words, "the word 'educated' actually refers to the speakers of this language, whereas the term 'formal' refers to the language itself". I agree with Ryding's criticism, but I will nevertheless use ESA because it has been widely used in the literature and I do not want to add to the many terms already circulating to refer to this variety.

3 Shiri (2013: 577) quotes a (non-Cornell) student in a study-abroad program in Tunisia who writes, "I didn't realize that learning Tunisian Arabic has helped me understand my friend's Saudi dialect upon returning home." This is another testimonial in support of the fact that students who learn one *'Āmmiyya* variety are able to communicate with speakers of another variety.

4 Parkinson informed me that he no longer feels the same way about this issue (personal communication, June 1992),

5 To this effect, Al-Batal (1992: 302) writes: "the confusion that will be felt by the students should be regarded as part of the total experience of learning Arabic. This confusion is a reflection of what native speakers of Arabic experience when they start their formal study of MSA. It is a product of the diglossic situation and is experienced not only by speakers of Arabic, but by speakers of all diglossic languages. Therefore, teachers should be prepared to deal with this confusion and should make it clear to the students that the level of confusion will gradually diminish as they become more proficient in the language. Teachers should also tolerate the mixing of MSA and the dialect in contexts where mixing would not be expected. We should always bear in mind that the appropriate mixing of the different varieties in Arabic is a skill in its own right and should be treated as such."

6 Conclusion

The main thesis of this book can be summed up as follows: for an AFL program to be successful it must meet the needs of its students in the most efficient manner. Surveys of Arabic student needs and goals over the past quarter century have consistently shown that they are focused on the desire to learn Arabic in order to understand, speak, read, and write it as it is understood, spoken, read, and written in real life by native speakers. These native speakers use a *ʿĀmmiyya* variety for conversation and *Fuṣḥā* for reading, writing and scripted speech. So the task of AFL programs should be straightforward: introducing both varieties of the language in a way that reflects native usage. Yet, the practice is radically different in the overwhelming majority of programs, where the focus is solely or primarily on *Fuṣḥā*. *ʿĀmmiyya* plays a very minor role, if any.

A number of justifications have traditionally been given as an explanation for this state of affairs, such as lack of proper instructional materials, the multiplicity of the *ʿĀmmiyya* varieties as opposed to the universality of *Fuṣḥā*, and fear of confusing students, among others. I have argued in the previous chapters that none of the problems typically raised are insurmountable and that the justification for the continuation of the status quo lies in the privileged status of *Fuṣḥā* and the stigmatization of *ʿĀmmiyya*. For real change to take place in AFL programs this deeply entrenched attitude about the two varieties of the language, of equal importance to the foreign learner, needs to change. There are clear signs that such change has begun. The results of the Abdalla and Al-Batal survey of Arabic teachers (2011–12) quoted in Chapter 3 clearly show that there is more recognition of the importance of *ʿĀmmiyya* than before among Arabic teachers. There is

> a noticeable change in the Arabic field … [where] there is acceptance of the principle [of integrating colloquial Arabic] among Arabic teachers, the majority of whom (over 65 percent) strongly agree or agree that training in a dialect should start at the early stages of instruction.
>
> (Ibid.: 16)

The driving force behind this change is likely to be the fact that more Arabic students are able to travel to the Arab world and interact with Arabs than ever before. These students report their frustrations at their inability to function successfully in Arabic after many years of study within the traditional framework in which they are taught to use *Fuṣḥā* for conversation.

Once this basic structural problem has been properly addressed, Arabic will be able to assume its rightful place among the major world languages in the field of foreign language study. Its rich history, direct relevance in the lives of over one billion Muslims, importance of the Arab world not only in terms of its strategic location straddling the three continents of Asia, Africa, and Europe but also in terms of its natural resources should put it on par, not with the less commonly taught foreign languages, but with the most commonly taught ones.

The perception that Arabic is a difficult or "superhard" language (Ryding 2006: 15) must have its roots in its diglossic nature. The Arabs themselves think of Arabic as a difficult language. By "Arabic", they, of course, mean *Fuṣḥā* and its grammar, with its particularly complicated rules of *'I'rāb* (Muṣṭafā 1959; Ḍayf 1986; Awzūn 2002). Arabic is not unique in having such a system. What is unique is that it is not used for conversation and thus is never acquired and reinforced as other features of the language are and as case and mood systems are acquired and reinforced in languages which have them such as German and Russian. An Arab with a high school education has no trouble reading Arabic, where the issue of *'I'rāb* plays a drastically diminished role. If the fiction that *Fuṣḥā* is used for ordinary conversation is abandoned, then much of the perceived difficulty disappears.

As has been shown in Chapter 4, one of the main features of the Integrated Approach to Arabic instruction is the use of *'Āmmiyya* for conversation, so the issue of using the case and mood system in conversation never arises and both the learner and the teacher use a system of communication that is actually used by native speakers.

References

Abboud, Peter. 1971. "State of the Art IX: Arabic Language Instruction". *Middle East Studies Association Bulletin* 5 (2), 1–23.

Abboud, Peter, Z. N. Abdel-Malek, N. A. Bezirgan, W. M. Erwin, M. A. Khouri, E. N. McCarus, R. M. Rammuny, and G. N. Saad. 1983. *Elementary Modern Standard Arabic*. Cambridge: Cambridge University Press.

Abd-el-Jawad, Hassan. 1986. "The Emergence of an Urban Dialect in the Jordanian Urban Centers". *International Journal of the Sociology of Language* 61 (1), 53–63.

——1987. "Cross-Dialectal Variation in Arabic: Competing Prestigious Forms". *Language in Society* 16 (3), 359–67.

Abdalla, Mahmoud and Mahmoud Al-Batal. 2011–12. "College-Level Teachers of Arabic in the United States: A Survey of Their Professional and Institutional Profiles and Attitudes". *Al-'Arabiyya* 44/45, 1–28.

Abdulaziz, Mohamed H. 1986. "Factors in the Development of Modern Arabic Usage". *International Journal of the Sociology of Language* 62, 11–24.

Abed, Shukri and Arwa Sawan. 2011. *Al-Madkhal: Spoken Standard Arabic*. New Haven and London: Yale University Press.

Al-Batal, Mahmoud. 1992. "Diglossia Proficiency: The Need for an Alternative Approach to Teaching". In *The Arabic Language in America*, Aleya Rouchdy (ed.). Detroit: Wayne State University Press, 284–304.

Al-Batal, Mahmoud and R. Kirk Belnap. 2006. "The Teaching and Learning of Arabic in the United States: Realities, Needs, and Future Directions". In *Handbook for Arabic Language Teaching Professionals in the 21st Century*, Kassem M. Wahba, Zeinab A. Taha and Liz England (eds). Mahwah, NJ: Lawrence Erlbaum Associates, 389–99.

Al-Hamad, Fayiz. 1983. "Problems in Teaching Arabic to Foreigners". In *Proceedings of the Second Annual Linguistics Conference*, Jonathan Owens and Issam Abu Salim (eds). Irbid, Jordan: Yarmouk University, 81–100.

Al-Khūlī, Amīn. 1987. *Mushkilāt ḥayātinā al-lughawīyah*. Cairo: al-Hay'ah al-Miṣriyyah al-'Āmmah lil-Kitāb.

Allen, Roger. 1989. "Arabic Proficiency Guidelines". *Foreign Language Annals* 22 (4), 373–92.

——1992. "Teaching Arabic in the United States: Past, Present and Future". In *The Arabic Language in America*, Aleya Rouchdy (ed.). Detroit: Wayne State University Press, 222–50.

Alosh, Mahdi. 1991. "Arabic Diglossia and Its Impact on Teaching Arabic as a Foreign Lanuage". In *International Perspectives on Foreign Language Teaching*, Gerard L. Ervin (ed.). Lincolnwood: National Textbook Company, 121–37.

——1992. "Designing a Proficiency-oriented Syllabus for Modern Standard Arabic as a Foreign Language". In *The Arabic Language in America*, Aleya Rouchdy (ed.). Detroit: Wayne State University Press, 251–83.

Awzūn, Zakariyyā. 2002. *Jināyat Sībawayh: al-rafḍ al-tāmm limā fī al-nahw min awhām* (Sībawayh's Crime: Total Refutation of the Myths of Arabic Syntax). Beirut: Riyad al-Rayyis li-al-Kutub wa-al-Nashr.

Badawi, El-Said. 1973. *Mustawayāt al-'Arabiyya al-mu'āSira fī miṣr* (Levels of Contemporary Arabic in Egypt). Cairo: Dār al-ma'ārif.

——1985. "Educated Spoken Arabic: A Problem in Teaching Arabic as a Second Language". In *Scientific and Humanistic Dimensions of Language: Festschrift for Robert Lado on the Occasion of his 70th Birthday on May 31, 1985,* Kurt R. Jankowsky (ed.). Amsterdam, Philadelphia: J. Benjamins, 15–22.

Bassiouney, Reem. 2006. *Functions of Code-Switching in Egypt: Evidence from Monologues.* Leiden, Boston: Brill.

——2009. *Arabic Sociolinguistics* [electronic resource]. Edinburgh: Edinburgh University Press. (Palo Alto, CA: ebrary, 2010).

Belnap, R. Kirk. 1987. "Who's Taking Arabic and What on Earth for? A Survey of Students in Arabic Language Programs". *Al-'Arabiyya* 20 (1/2), 29–42.

——2006. "A Profile of Students of Arabic in US Universities". In *Handbook for Arabic Language Teaching Professionals in the 21st Century*, Kassem M. Wahba, Zeinab A. Taha and Liz England (eds). Mahwah, NJ: Lawrence Erlbaum Associates.

Bishai, Wilson. 1966. "Modern Inter-Arabic". *Journal of the American Oriental Society* 86 (3), 319–23.

Blanc, Haim. 1960. "Stylistic Variations in Spoken Arabic: A Sample Inter-dialectal Educated Conversation". In *Contributions to Arabic Linguistics*, Charles Ferguson (ed.). Harvard Middle Eastern Monograph, No. 3. Cambridge, MA: Harvard University Press, 79–161.

Brustad, Kristin, Mahmoud Al-Batal, and Abbas Al-Tonsi. 2004 [1995]. *Al-Kitaab fii Ta'allum al-'Arabiyya.* Washington, DC: Georgetown University Press.

Cachia, P. J. E. 1967. "The Use of the Colloquial in Modern Arabic Literature". *Journal of the American Oriental Society* 87 (1), 12–22.

Cadora, Frederic. 1965. "The Teaching of Spoken and Written Arabic". *Language Learning* 15 (3/4), 133–6.

——1976. "Lexical Relationships Among Arabic Dialects and the Swadesh List". *Anthropological Linguistics* 18 (6), 235–60.

——1979. *Interdialectal Lexical Compatibility in Arabic: An Analytical Study of the Lexical Relationships among the Major Syro-Lebanese Varieties.* Leiden: Brill.

Dawwārah, Fu'ād. 1996. *'Asharat 'Udabā' Yataḥaddathūn.* Cairo: Maṭābi' al-Hay'a al-Miṣriyya al-'āmma li-l-Kitāb.

Ḍayf, Shawqī. 1986. *Taysīr al-Naḥw al-Ta'līmī Qadīman wa Hadīthan* (Simplifying School Grammar, Past and the Present). Cairo: Dar al-Ma'ārif.

El-Hassan, Shaher. 1977. "Educated Spoken Arabic in Egypt and the Levant: A Critical Review of Diglossia and Related Concepts". *Archivum Linguisticum* 8 (2), 112–32.

——1978. "Variation in the Demonstrative System in Educated Spoken Arabic". *Archivum Linguisticum* 9 (1), 32–57.

Elverskog, Liljana. 1999. *Verb Morphology in Educated Spoken Arabic.* Ann Arbor, Michigan: UMI Dissertation Services.

Encyclopedia Britannica Online. German Language. At: www.britannica.com (accessed 13 February 2014).

Ezzat, Ali. 1974. *Intelligibility Among Arabic Dialects.* Beirut: Beirut Arab University.
Ferguson, Charles. 1959. "Diglossia". *Word* 15, 325–40
——1971. "Problems of Teaching Languages with Diglossia". In *Language Structure and Language Use*, Anwar S. Dil (ed.). Stanford, Calif.: Stanford University Press, 71–86. Originally published in 1962 in *The Georgetown University Monograph Series on Languages and Linguistics*, Monograph No. 15, Washington, DC: Georgetown University Press, 165–77.
——1996. "Epilogue: Diglossia Revisited". In *Understanding Arabic: Essays in Contemporary Arabic Linguistics in Honor of El-Said Badawi*, Alā Elgibali (ed.). Cairo: American University in Cairo Press.
Haddad, Surayya. 1985. "Tadrīs al-mahaaraat al-shafawiyya: mawqif jadīd". *Al-'Arabiyya* 18 (1/2), 15–21.
Heath, Peter. 1990. "Proficiency in Arabic Language Learning: Some Reflections on Basic Goals". *Al-'Arabiyya* 23 (1/2), 31–48.
Holes, Clive. 2004. *Modern Arabic: Structures, Functions, and Varieties.* Washington, DC: Georgetown University Press.
Hussein, R. and N. El-Ali. 1989. "Subjective Reactions of Rural University Students towards Different Varieties of Arabic". *Al-'Arabiyya* 22, 37–54.
Husseinali, Ghassan. 2006. "Who is Studying Arabic and Why? A Survey of Arabic Students' Orientations at a Major University". *Foreign Language Annals* 39 (3), 395–412.
Ibrahim, Muhammad. (1986). "Standard and Prestige Language: a Problem in Arabic Linguistics". *Anthropological Linguistics* 28 (1), 115–26.
Kaye, Alan S. 1972. "Remarks on Diglossia in Arabic: Well-defined vs. Ill-defined". *Linguistics* 81: 32–48.
Lampe, Gerald. 1985. "Ta 'līm al-Mahaaraat al-shafawiyya li al-lugha al-'Arabiyya". *Al-'Arabiyya* 18 (1/2), 11–14.
Mansoor, Menahem. 1960. "Arabic: What and When to Teach". In *Report of the Tenth Annual Round Table Meeting on Linguistics and Language Studies*, Richard Harrel (ed.). Washington, DC: Georgetown University Press, 83–96.
McCarus, Ernest. 1992. "A History of Arabic Study in the United States". In *The Arabic Language in America.* Aleya Rouchdy (ed.). Detroit: Wayne State University Press, 207–21.
Meiseles, Gustav. (1980). "Educated Spoken Arabic and the Arabic Language Continuum". *Archivum Linguisticum* 11 (2), 118–48.
Mejdell, Gunvor. 2006. *Mixed styles in spoken Arabic in Egypt: Somewhere Between Order and Chaos.* Leiden, Boston: Brill.
Mitchell, T. F. 1975. "Some Preliminary Observations on the Arabic Koine". *Bulletin of the British Society for Middle Eastern Studies* 2 (2), 70–86.
——1978. "Educated Spoken Arabic in Egypt and the Levant, with Special Reference to Participle and Tense". *Journal of Linguistics* 14 (2), 227–58
——1980. "Dimensions of Style in a Grammar of Educated Spoken Arabic". *Archivum Linguisticum* 11 (2), 89–106.
——(1986). " What is Educated Spoken Arabic?". *International Journal of the Sociology of Language* 61: 7–32.
——1990. "The Mixture Not as Before". In *Diglossic Tension: Teaching Arabic for Communication*, Dionisius A. Agius (ed.). Leeds: Folia Scholastica, 18–26.
Mitchell, T. F. and S. A. al-Hassan. 1994. *Modality, Mood, and Aspect in Spoken Arabic: With Special Reference to Egypt and the Levant.* London; New York: Kegan Paul International.

Muṣṭafā, Ibrāhīm. 1959. *Ihyā' al-naḥw* (Bringing Syntax Back to Life). Cairo: Maṭba'at Lajnat al-Ta'līf wa-al-Tarjama wa-al-Nashr.
Nicola, Michel. 1990. "Starting Arabic with Dialect". In *Diglossic Tension: Teaching Arabic for Communication*, Dionisius A. Agius (ed.). Leeds: Folia Scholastica, 42–5.
Palmer, Jeremy. 2007. "Arabic Diglossia: Teaching Only the Standard Variety Is a Disservice to Students". *Arizona Working Papers in SLA & Teaching* 14, 111–22.
Parkinson, Dilworth. 1985. "Proficiency to Do What? Developing Proficiency in Students of Modern Standard Arabic". *Al-'Arabiyya* 18 (1/2), 11–44.
Rammuny, Raji. 1993. "Interview with Professor Ernest McCarus (in Arabic)" in *American Association of Teachers of Arabic (AATA) Newsletter*, February 1993.
Ryding, Karin. 1991. "Proficiency Despite Diglossia: A New Approach for Arabic". *The Modern Language Journal* 75 (2), 212–18.
——2006. "Teaching Arabic in the United States". In *Handbook for Arabic Language Teaching Professionals in the 21st Century*, Kassem M. Wahba, Zeinab A. Taha and Liz England (eds). Mahwah, NJ: Lawrence Erlbaum Associates, 13–20.
Sa'īd, Naffūsa Z. 1964. *Tārīkh al-Da'wa ilā al-''āmmiyya wa 'āthāruhā fī Miṣr* (The History of Calling for [the use of] 'āmmiyya and its Effects in Egypt). Alexandrai, Egypt: Dār Nashr al-Thaqāfa.
Sallam, A. M. 1980. "Phonological Variation in Educated Spoken Arabic". *Bulletin of the School of Oriental and African Studies* 43, 77–100.
Sawaie, Muhammad. 2006. "Language Academies". In *Encyclopedia of Arabic Language and Linguistics Online.* Lemma in K. Versteegh, M. Eid, A. Elgibali, M. Woidich and A. Zaborski (eds). Leiden: Brill.
Shiri, Sonia. 2002. "Speak Arabic Please! Tunisian Arabic Speakers' Linguistic Accommodation to Middle Easterners". In *Language Contact and Language Conflict in Arabic: Variations on a Sociolinguistic Theme*, Aleya Rouchdy (ed.). London: Curzon, 149–74.
——2013. "Learners' Attitudes toward Regional Dialects and Destination Preferences in Study Abroad". *Foreign Language Annals* 46 (4), 565–87.
Versteegh, Kees. 2006. "History of Arabic Language Teaching". In *Handbook for Arabic Language Teaching Professionals in the 21st Century*, Kassem M. Wahba, Zeinab A. Taha and Liz England (eds), Mahwah, NJ: Lawrence Erlbaum Associates, 3–12.
Williams, Malcolm. 1990. "Ordering the Teaching of Arabic". In *Diglossic Tension: Teaching Arabic for Communication*, Dionisius A. Agius (ed.). Leeds: Folia Scholastica, 46–49.
Wilmsen, David. 2006. "What is Communicative Arabic?". In *Handbook for Arabic Language Teaching Professionals in the 21st Century*, Kassem M. Wahba, Zeinab A. Taha and Liz England (eds). Mahwah, NJ: Lawrence Erlbaum Associates, 125–38.
Younes, Munther. 1990. "An Integrated Approach to Teaching Arabic as a Foreign Language". *Al-'Arabiyya* 23 (1/2), 105–22.
——1995a. "An Integrated Curriculum for Elementary Arabic". In *The Teaching of Arabic as a Foreign Language: Issues and Directions* (*Al-'Arabiyya* Monograph Series No. 2), Mahmoud al-Batal (ed.), 233–55.
——1995b. *Elementary Arabic: An Integrated Approach.* New Haven and London: Yale University Press.
——1995c. Review of *Levantine Arabic for Non-natives: A Proficiency-oriented Approach* by Lutfi Hussein. *Al-'Arabiyya* 28, 161–6.
——1999. *Intermediate Arabic: An Integrated Approach.* New Haven and London: Yale University Press.

——2006. "Integrating the Colloquial with *Fusha* in the Arabic-as-a-Foreign-Language Classroom". In *Handbook for Arabic Language Teaching Professionals in the 21st Century*, Kassem M. Wahba, Zeinab A. Taha and Liz England (eds). Mahwah, NJ: Lawrence Erlbaum Associates, 157–66.

Younes, Munther, Makda Weatherspoon and Maha Foster. 2014. *'Arabiyyat al-Naas (Part I): An Introductory Course in Arabic*. London and New York: Routledge.

Younes, Munther and Hanada al-Masri. 2014. *'Arabiyyat al-Naas (Part II): An Intermediate Course in Arabic*. London and New York: Routledge.

Younes, Munther and Yomna Chami. 2014. *'Arabiyyat al-Naas (Part III): An Advanced Course in Arabic*. London and New York: Routledge.

Zahrān, al-Badrāwi. 1989. "Izdiwājiyyat al-Lugha wa Ḍarūrat Rasm Siyāsa Lughawiyya" (Diglossia and the Necessity to Chart a Language Policy). *Majallat Majma' al-Lugha al-'Arabiyya* 65, 89–112.

Zughoul, Muhammad. 1980. "Diglossia in Arabic: Investigating Solutions". *Anthropological Linguistics* 22 (5), 201–17.

Index

Abboud, Peter 16, 23, 26, 31, 45
Abdalla, Mahmoud 57
Abed, Shukri 47
AFL *see* Arabic as a foreign language
Al-Batal, Mahmoud 32, 37, 45, 49, 56, 57
Al-Hamad, Fayiz 46–47
Al-Kitaab fii Ta'allum al-'Arabiyya (Brustad et al.) 16, 23, 55
Allen, Roger 23
'Āmmiyya: acquisition by native speakers 4; Badawi's levels of 6–7; choosing which dialect to teach 46–47, 49–51, 54; as Ferguson's 'L' (low) 2–5; grammar 4, 39–40, 43–44; in Modern Inter-Arabic 8–9; mutual intelligibility 19; pecking order of prestige within 20; problems of teaching 27–28; seen as divisive 18–19, 20, 27; seen as Western conspiracy 27; shared features with *Fuṣḥā* 38–39, 40–42; use of term 17; variation in 4, 27, 28, 37, 46–47; writing 37; *see also* Integrated Approach; intermediate linguistic varieties; Levantine Educated Spoken Arabic
'Āmmiyya al-muthaqqafīn 6, 11, 47
Arabic: considered a difficult language 58; importance of 58; intermediate varieties 5–12, 19; *see also* *'Āmmiyya*; *Fuṣḥā*
Arabic as a foreign language (AFL): dominant pattern 26; early study of 22; in Europe 23–24; motivations for studying 24–25, 30; in USA 22–23
Arabic Language Academy, Damascus 27
'Arabiyyat al-Naas (Younes et al.) 32–33, 34, 38, 42, 54
Arem, Jacob 52
Army Language School, Monterey 5–6

Badawi, El-Said 6–7, 10, 11, 42, 48–49
Bassiouney, Reem 15, 20–21, 27
Belnap, R. Kirk 24, 49
Bishai, Wilson 8–9, 20
Blanc, Haim 5–6, 10, 11
British rule: in Egypt 27

Cadora, Frederic 8, 13–14
Cairo Arabic 9, 13
Casa Blanca Arabic 13, 14
Classical Arabic 3, 6, 9, 13, 17, 22; *see also Fuṣḥā*
classicizing 6, 19
classroom environment 42–43
colloquial Arabic *see 'Āmmiyya*
Columbia University 23
confusion, students' 54–56
continuum concept 12
conversation 3, 5, 6, 17, 28–30, 49, 57; educated 9, 18–19; in Integrated Approach 33–34, 42–44, 50, 52; as motivation for studying AFL 24, 25; use of *Fuṣḥā* 42–43, 55, 58
Cornell University 32, 33, 47, 49, 50–53, 54
Cunha, Priscilla 51

Damascus 9, 27
Defense Language Institute, US 22, 31
dialect-neutrality 50
differences, linguistic 10, 13, 34, 40; *see also* variation, linguistic
diglossia: defined 2; Ferguson on 2–5; Ferguson's analysis challenged 5–12, 14–15; German 15; stability 4

Educated Arabic (EA) 14
Educated Spoken Arabic (ESA) 10–11, 12, 16, 31; Badawi on teaching 48–49; criticism of term 56; Elverskog on 14; lack of codification 11, 49; Meiseles on 7, 8; mutual intelligibility 19; previous attempts to teach 47–48; *see also* Levantine Educated Spoken Arabic
education, role of 14, 17–19
Egypt: British rule 27; use of ESA 10, 14, 19; usefulness of Levantine Arabic in 51, 52
Egyptian Arabic 6–7, 23–24, 40, 41, 46, 47, 49–50, 55; Cairo 9, 13; sub-dialects 18
Egyptian Colloquial Arabic (ECA) 27, 51
El-Hassan, Shaher 10
Elementary Modern Standard Arabic (Abboud et al.) 16
Elverskog, Liljana 11, 14
English language: varieties 9, 37, 53
Ezzat, Ali 13, 14

Fan, Ryan 52
Ferguson, Charles: challenges to 5–12, 14–15; on instability in Arabic 11; on intermediate forms 12; on language maintenance 43; "Diglossia" 2–5, 11, 42, 45
Foreign Service Institute, US 22, 48
Formal Spoken Arabic (FSA) 9–10, 48
four language skills 25, 33, 44
Fuṣḥā: acquisition 4; compared to High German 15; difficulty of using for conversation 42–43, 55, 58; Egyptian 6–7; as Ferguson's 'H' (high) 2–5; function 3; grammar 4, 38, 39–40, 42, 43–44, 48–49; interactions with *'Āmmiyya* 5–12, 17–18, 42–43; *I'rāb* system 20, 33, 49, 58; lexicon 5, 9, 18, 36; literary heritage 3; Meiseles on 7–8; as only legitimate written form 2, 10–11, 16, 37–38; prestige 3, 20, 26–27; reasons for and consequences of privileging 26–30; reasons for learning 25, 26; religious dimension 15, 20, 26–27; renamed as *Faṣīḥ* 47, 49; shared features with *'Āmmiyya* 38–39, 40–42; stability 4, 38; standardization 4; as unifier 18–19, 20, 39; US studies 22, 23; use of term 17; *see also* Classical Arabic; Modern Standard Arabic

German language 13, 15, 58; High German 15; Swiss 2, 15
Gillen, Ian 52
grammar: *'Āmmiyya*/LESA 4, 35–36, 39–40, 42, 43–44, 49; ESA and MSA compared 10; *Fuṣḥā* 4, 38, 39–40, 42, 43–44, 48–49; lack of codification in ESA 11, 49
Greek language 2, 15

Haddad, Surayya 9, 47–48
Haitian Creole 2, 15
Holes, Clive 12, 13
Husseinali, Ghassan 24

Ibrahim, Muhammad 9, 15, 19, 37, 49
immigrants, Arab 23
Integrated Approach (IA) 31–45; advantages of 38–44; basic description and rationale 32–33; implementation 33–34; increased acceptance of 57–58; objections to 46–56; *see also* Levantine Educated Spoken Arabic
Intercommon Spoken Arabic (ISA) 8
intermediate linguistic varieties 5–12, 19
internet 17
I'rāb system 20, 33, 49, 58
Iraqi Arabic 13, 40, 52, 54

Jerusalem Arabic 6, 9
Jidda Arabic 13
Jordan 29, 33–34, 47, 51, 52–53

Koppelman, Emily 53
Krashen, Stephen 31

laysa, forms of 43–44
Leeds, University of 10
Levantine Educated Spoken Arabic (LESA) 10, 19, 33, 34–38, 41; as choice of dialect for teaching 46, 47, 49–51, 54; lexicon 36; morphology 35; phonology 35; possessive pronouns 39–40; relationship with *Fuṣḥā* 41–42; sub-dialects 18; syntax 36; textbook 54; writing 37–38
leveling 6, 19
lexicon 5, 9, 18, 36; *see also* vocabulary
linguistic investigation: versus pedagogical need 41, 47

Maghribi colloquial varieties 14, 50
Mahfouz, Naguib 27
Mashriqi colloquial varieties 14
materials, instructional 43
media: *Fuṣḥā* as language of 18, 38; news broadcasts 3, 25, 43; role of 14
Meiseles, Gustav 7–8, 10, 19
Mejdell, Gunvor 12, 17, 18
Middlebury College: Arabic Summer School 23
Mitchell, T. F. 8, 10–11, 15, 20
Modern Inter-Arabic 8–9
Modern Standard Arabic (MSA) 8, 10–11, 12; Badawi on teaching 48–49; Integrated Approach and 31–32; limitations of 28–30, 51; oral reinforcement in 30; as problematic term 16–17; studied in USA and Europe 23–24, 26; taught concurrently with FSA 48
Moroccan Arabic 13, 14, 18, 37, 50
mutual intelligibility 13–14, 19, 49

negation 43–44
news broadcasts 3, 25, 43
newspapers 18, 42, 43
Nicola, Michel 16–17, 31, 48

"Orange Books" 16, 23

Palestinian Arabic 6, 18, 35–36, 54
Palmer, Jeremy 24, 28–29
Parkinson, Dilworth 30, 54–55
pedagogical need: versus linguistic investigation 41, 47
possessive pronoun 39–40
prestige 3, 20, 26–27, 36
proficiency movement 24

Qur'ān 3, 15, 20, 22, 26

reverse privileging 29
Ryding, Karin 9–10, 29, 48, 56

Sawaie, Muhammad 27
Sawan, Arwa 47
Shiri, Sonia 25, 28, 29, 49–50, 53
Sībawayh 22, 38
sub-dialects 18
Substandard Arabic (SsA) 7–8
Supra-Dialectal Low (SDL) 9, 37–38, 47, 49
Syro-Lebanese colloquial varieties 13–14

Terrell, Tracy D. 31
Texas, University of 14
transliteration, Roman 37
Tunisian Arabic 8–9, 50, 56

United States of America: Arabic studies 22–23, 24, 29
urban dialects 6, 9, 13, 20, 35

variation, linguistic 41; in *'Āmmiyya* 4, 27, 28, 37, 46–47; *see also* differences, linguistic
vernacular Arabic 10, 11–12; *see also 'Āmmiyya*
Versteegh, Kees 23

Williams, Malcolm 30, 41
Wilmsen, David 11–12, 16–17, 30, 32
written Arabic 2, 10–11, 16, 28; in LESA 37–38; transliteration 37; *see also Fuṣḥā*

Younes, Munther 25, 26, 32, 37

Zahrān, al-Badrāwi 27
Zughoul, Muhammad 14

For Product Safety Concerns and Information please contact our EU representative GPSR@taylorandfrancis.com
Taylor & Francis Verlag GmbH, Kaufingerstraße 24, 80331 München, Germany

www.ingramcontent.com/pod-product-compliance
Lightning Source LLC
Chambersburg PA
CBHW070742230426
43669CB00014B/2542
* 9 7 8 1 1 3 8 8 2 2 3 2 0 *